EDUCATION MATTERS

General Editor: Ted Wragg

HIGHER EDUCATION

HIGHER
EDUCATION

Donald Bligh

CASSELL

Cassell Educational Limited
Villiers House
41/47 Strand
London WC2N 5JE
England

© Cassell Educational Limited 1990

First published 1990

British Library Cataloguing in Publication Data
Bligh, Donald, *1936-*
  Higher education – (Education matters).
  1. Great Britain. Higher education
  I. Title   II. Series
  378.41

ISBN 0–304–31954–6 (hardback)
      0–304–31959–7 (paperback)

Phototypeset by Input Typesetting, London

Printed and bound in Great Britain by
Biddles Ltd, Guildford and King's Lynn

CONTENTS

FOREWORD

Professor E. C. Wragg, Exeter University

During the 1980s a succession of Education Acts changed considerably the nature of schools and their relationships with the outside world. Parents were given more rights and responsibilities, including the opportunity to serve on the governing body of their child's school. The 1988 Education Reform Act in particular, by introducing for the first time a National Curriculum, the testing of children at the ages of 7, 11, 14 and 16, local management, including financial responsibility and the creation of new types of school, was a radical break with the past. Furthermore the disappearance of millions of jobs, along with other changes in our society, led to reforms not only of schools, but also of further and higher education.

In the wake of such rapid and substantial changes it was not just parents and lay people, but also teachers and other professionals working in education, who found themselves struggling to keep up with what these many changes meant and how to get the best out of them. The *Education Matters* series addresses directly the major topics of reform, such as the new curriculum, testing and assessment, the role of parents and the handling of school finances, considering their effects on primary, secondary, further and higher education, and also the continuing education of adults.

The aim of the series is to present information about the challenges facing education in the remainder of the twentieth century in an authoritative but readable form. The books in the series, therefore, are of particular interest to parents, governors and all those concerned with education, but are written in such a way as to give an overview to students, experienced teachers and other professionals who work in the field.

Each book gives an account of the relevant legislation and background, but, more importantly, stresses practical implications of change with specific examples of what is being or can be done to make reforms work effectively. The authors are not only authorities in their field, but also have direct experience of the matters they write about. That is why the *Education Matters* series makes an important contribution to both debate and practice.

INTRODUCTION

This book is for those people who have not experienced higher education and who now need to know about it. They include parents whose children will benefit from it, and employers who will work with students and academics.

It is also for parents, teachers, careers advisers and others who have experienced higher education but have not kept abreast of the changes. But it is not another guide for intending applicants. The ideas and information brought together in this book will not be found in college prospectuses or university brochures.

When change is rapid we easily forget fundamental principles and things of lasting value. This book presents a reminder.

The time when children first go to college can be an anxious one for parents. So many things seem uncertain. When the vacation comes the children seem different – they are no longer dependent. Advice is no longer appropriate. That is not surprising. Education is intended to change people.

More understanding is needed. That is why this book is about understanding higher education and the people engaged in it.

It is intended as a book for lay men and women, but every Vice-Chancellor and polytechnic director will find a few things they did not know. Chapter 1 represents some misunderstandings of people I have met who were unfamiliar with higher education. Chapters 2 and 3 form a basis for what follows, but on the whole you can read any chapter independently. So if you just want to dip in here and there, go ahead. You should find that the sub-headings help you.

I have tried to write simply without over-simplifying, but some subjects, like academic freedom, require a lot of thought no matter how simply they are expressed. What I have written depends a great deal upon research, but to make reading easier I have deliberately not flooded the text with references to the original reports. Also for ease of reading, in some places I have used the male gender to stand for both sexes, but I realise that 44 per cent of students in higher education are women.

I am grateful to Ted Wragg for his comments on my first draft. I am also grateful to Cynthia Holme of Universities Statistical Record and to Sarita Presland of the Open University for use of their data. I know some people find statistics difficult. If you are one of them, skip-read and you should find that the tone of the text will give you the general meaning, even if not the detail.

Donald Bligh
1990

Chapter 1

POPULAR MISCONCEPTIONS

You get long holidays

It is early July. 'So you'll soon be on holiday until October' shouts my neighbour across the fence. He thinks that university dons sit around drinking all day, rather as they are sometimes depicted in television drama. I have explained to him before that people in universities spend half their time doing research. He says it partly to rile me and partly because he doesn't believe me, even though he knows when I go to work and when I come back.

You have one job, not two

He forgets that I have two jobs, teaching and research, to say nothing of the administration that goes with them. When he thinks of one, he overlooks the other. Yet his blind spot is curious. He works in industry. He is an intelligent man. If he had been born a generation later, he would have gone to university himself. As it is, he goes back indoors and looks at the News, *Tomorrow's World*, science and nature programmes, and other television programmes in which academics speak about their work. He is interested, even enthusiastic, about his company's latest research contract with the University. He is impressed by the advances in modern medicine. He is touched by the care and understanding shown by researchers in child abuse, dyslexia, and other social problems. Yet he doesn't associate any of this with the institution down the road. It's in quite a different compartment of his mind, because he assumes higher education is like school.

Higher education is like school

There is a gap in his experience. He has been to school and thinks that higher education is like secondary education, only a bit more difficult. He has never had the experience to know anything different. So what else can he think? How could he know what goes on at a university or a polytechnic? He confuses 'education' with 'schooling'. So he thinks higher education is like school learning, and colleges are like schools. But the relationship between academics and their students is quite different from that between schoolteachers and their pupils. There is greater mutual respect. They are both adults.

My neighbour tends to think that all students come straight from school. The majority still do. But 45 per cent of undergraduates are over 19 when they first enter university. In 1988, 14 per cent were over 21, 7 per cent were over 25, and 41 per cent of new postgraduates were over 25. The percentages in polytechnics are higher and they are rising quite fast.

Sadly, too many students today pass through higher education without understanding how it should be different from school, without being aware of the research that is going on around them, or realising the contribution being made to the nation and the community by an institution at the cutting edge of new knowledge. So perhaps I should not blame my neighbour too much.

Yet the spirit of enquiry that drives research should make higher education totally different from school. The attitudes towards knowledge and those who profess to know, are quite different. It's an attitude of challenging, testing and criticising the accepted 'truths' of the day.

Students are irresponsible libertines

There is another thing my neighbour doesn't understand. When at school, children are dependent upon their teachers and parents. Higher education cultivates independence of mind. Students must learn to think for themselves. I am quite delighted when I see my students marching in protest at something, organising a rag for charity, or going on a sponsored walk. Whether I agree with their protest, or whether they support my favourite charity is unimportant. At least they

4

care. They are not apathetic. They are thinking for themselves. They are challenging those of us in positions of influence to justify what we do and think. If they cannot be enthusiastic when young, what are they going to be like when they have to be respectable in middle age?

Higher education is the first opportunity my students have had to explore and work out their own values, in particular those concerned with religion, politics and personal relationships. It's the first time they are free from the constraints of home and school. For many students the most important thing they take away from college is a clearer understanding of themselves and the principles by which they will live.

My neighbour has an image of students going to bed with each other in rotation. He is quite mistaken. Considering their time of life and the close community life that they lead, students are a particularly responsible group. (Try comparing them with businessmen or even politicians!) But even supposing my neighbour is not entirely mistaken, if you don't hold a dogmatic view about what is right and wrong for all men and women, you should allow students some leeway to explore these issues for themselves. It would be hypocritical if college authorities said to their students, 'You should come to college to learn to think for yourself and to seek the truth in an open-minded and honest way; but we insist that your morality should be the same as ours'.

My neighbour cannot understand the fact that I not only tolerate, but even encourage, students to explore opinions and beliefs I do not myself hold, and may not even understand. He went to a school where the rules were laid down, principally by the headmaster. Facts and morals were given a spurious and dogmatic certainty. Consequently my neighbour cannot understand, and cannot tolerate, a community where these things are accepted as uncertain and open to doubt and scrutiny.

The truth is that higher education is at the forefront of change. Men and women live by their ideas, and those ideas change the world. But change is threatening. It threatens those in power and it threatens those who have to change with it. Because change produces uncertainty and uncertainty makes us feel insecure, there are established powerful forces that will not welcome the products of higher education, particularly those ideas that challenge established values. To my neighbour science and engineering are acceptable. He can use them without being disturbed in himself. But a challenge to change his values is another matter.

It is all theory, not practical

The very fact that my neighbour is unsettled by a challenge to his values shows that the challenge is a very practical one. It is so practical that my neighbour wants to avoid the challenge by saying, 'It's all irrelevant and theoretical'.

The challenge is part of the democratic process. Higher education is part of that process. Education is necessarily political. Politics is the use of power by taking decisions. The decisions depend upon knowledge, ideas and the capacity to think using them. These things are acquired in higher education. That is why universities have long been the seedbed of politics. But my neighbour thinks that education, politics, and religion should somehow be kept in separate watertight compartments. He hasn't understood that all knowledge is interconnected. You can't separate these things.

It's strange he should think that, because he also thinks everything we teach should be practical and relevant to modern life. But as soon as the students in history and sociology start relating what they've learnt to the contemporary world, he thinks they should get off the streets and get back to their books. He was taught history as a series of facts, not as a series of decisions raising fundamental principles and not as an appreciation of how other people think.

He contrasts theory and practice. In the back of his mind are sentences like: 'That's all very well in theory, but it won't work in practice'. The contrast is a mistake. There are good theories and bad theories; and good theories are very practical. He doesn't think of new designs for his company's product as speculations or hypotheses; but, until they are tested in practice, they are just as hypothetical as models in university economics or engineering departments.

He thinks that, just as many of his colleagues have been

with his company all their working lives, academics have always been academics and have no practical experience outside an ivory tower. He is quite wrong. Academics average about ten years' experience in industry, commerce or the professions before entering academia. Indeed, if they averaged much more than that, colleges could be accused of appointing staff past their most creative years and forming a generation gap between teachers and their students.

Higher education sponges on the taxpayer

My neighbour thinks that higher education sponges on the taxpayer. He has a simple argument: 'All the nation's wealth comes from those who make things and sell them, namely from agriculture and manufacturing industry. Services, like education, are financed from either Income Tax, VAT or other taxes on those who produce things. People in industry and agriculture don't owe educationalists a living.' He thinks parents should pay. The short answer to the last point is that they do, but his misconception is more fundamental.

It is true that all economic activities are ultimately dependent upon primary production, but it doesn't follow from that, that service industries and other activities make no contribution to the economy; quite the contrary. The enormous advances in agriculture and industry have been dependent upon research and inventions in institutions of higher education. My neighbour will deny that by pointing out, quite rightly, that his company employs researchers of its own. But he fails to appreciate that those researchers obtained their skills in the education system. Furthermore, they use knowledge from basic research that no company would ever have sponsored. The fundamentals of laser technology were discovered by a physicist playing with basic ideas. He did not sit down and say 'Now I am going to invent laser technology'. Advances in fundamental knowledge are not made like that.

My neighbour has a much more fundamental misunderstanding about how advances in knowledge are made. He underestimates their inter-disciplinary nature. Companies do not employ researchers in a wide range of disciplines on the off-chance that they will cross-fertilise each other to produce

7

ideas that might be relevant to their particular product. It would be foolish for hundreds of thousands of companies to employ researchers in fields not obviously relevant to their work just hoping that they might interact creatively in a way that happens to be useful. It would be inappropriate for companies to act independently in this way. What is needed are a number of institutions where researchers from a wide range of disciplines can work together, exchanging ideas and building up a resource of knowledge, available nationally, when it is needed. In other words, industry and the nation requires inter-disciplinary research institutions.

That is precisely what universities and polytechnics are. If we didn't have them, we would have to re-invent them. It would be inefficient to do research any other way. Yet there was widespread belief in industry that universities were inefficient (until the Jarratt Committee showed that they are not – see Chapter 4).

Only students and their parents benefit from higher education

Institutions of higher education are national resources of knowledge. (They are not the only ones: libraries, museums and, increasingly, databases also store knowledge for use when needed.) So it would be quite wrong to suppose that parents are the only people who benefit from their children receiving higher education. The same is true of school education. It would be foolish to suggest that only parents benefit from their children being able to read and write. The whole of our society is organised on the assumption that most people can. Our levels of literacy are a national resource. It is knowledge in people's minds that can be used. The same is true of the knowledge, ideas and thinking skills bestowed by higher education. It would therefore be quite wrong to suggest that parents alone should pay for their children's higher education. Everyone would be the poorer without it. The nation should pay to ensure that those who are capable of acquiring the skills demanded by higher education should do so, so that we all can benefit. The intelligence of our young people is a national resource and it is the nation that should invest in it. It is therefore quite right that the taxpayer should do so.

So what's higher education really like?

Actually my neighbour never asks this question. I am glad about that, because it would be a bit difficult to tell him over the garden fence. I would have to tell him that higher education has several different purposes (Chapter 2). Sometimes they're incompatible.

Like his company, higher education is the way it is (Chapter 4), because of its history (Chapter 3). But, unlike his company, it's got a mighty long history, and many of the factors that influenced that history are abstract ideas.

The students we get also influence what higher education is like (Chapters 5 and 6). So do the methods of teaching and learning, research and assessment (Chapters 7, 8 and 9). Finally, as in any other organisation, the management and finance of colleges (Chapters 10 and 11), together with the staff they employ (Chapter 12), influence what higher education is really like.

I will look at each of these in turn, but the chapters don't have to be read in that order. You can dip in more or less where you like. If you don't understand something because I dealt with it in an earlier chapter, the Index will tell you where to find it explained.

Further reading

Sir Christopher Ball and Heather Eggins (eds), *Higher Education into the 1990s – new dimensions* (Society for Research into Higher Education, 1989).

Chapter 2

WHAT IS HIGHER EDUCATION FOR?

I. To develop attitudes and emotional adjustment

Education is primarily about emotions. Imagine your child has Down's syndrome, spina bifida or some other handicap. Your main concern will not be that he or she should go to university, or get a degree, or even be able to live a normal life. Your most important aim will be that he or she will have a happy life even if it is not a very long one. Happiness is a collection of emotions.

When the chips are down, what is most important in life is to love and be loved; to trust and be trusted; to have self-esteem and the esteem of others; to have self-confidence and to impart it; and to be honest, hard-working and responsible.

These things have more to do with the emotions than the intellect, more to do with feelings than thoughts, more to do with attitudes than knowledge. The American social psychologist Stanley Milgram was asked to study why apparently decent middle-class young men could stab a Vietnamese baby twenty times. He found that these young men had experienced fear and obedience to authority in their childhood and adolescence. Their motivation emerged from repressed aggression, punishments and the emotional stresses that they suffered as children. The same was true of ordinary citizens in Germany and Austria before the Second World War, yet no one recognised it. There are similar repressions in our own society, not least where discipline is strongly enforced in our schools.

A warm, caring and stable environment during early childhood produces a well-adjusted and sociable adult; fear results in aggression later. Yet the government's proposals for curricula and assessment in schools not only ignore these priorities, they militate against them. Tests of academic performance at 7, 11 and 14 years of age will pressure teachers to use a didactic authoritarian style and to neglect the education of the emotions.

Fear breeds intolerance. That is inimical to higher education. The more we know about the emotional development of children and young people, the more important the earliest years of childhood appear to be. Yet there is little or nothing on parenthood in the new National Curriculum.

These defects in school education must affect the aims of higher education. Colleges can no longer assume that they are recruiting well-rounded, well-adjusted individuals. To compensate for the defects of government legislation, the education of the emotions must become a major aim of higher education. Higher education is no longer a supplement to basic education. It must attend to the basics itself.

No account of the aims of higher education in Britain would be complete without mentioning the four aims given by the Robbins Committee in 1963:

- instruction in occupational skills (develop the nation's economy);
- to promote the general powers of the mind (develop the intellect of the individual);
- the advancement of learning (develop knowledge); and
- the transmission of a common culture and common standards of citizenship (develop society).

Do these aims conflict? What are the priorities? Let's consider each of them in turn.

II. To provide a base of adaptable occupational skills

The government thinks that instruction in occupational skills is by far the most important. The White Paper of April 1987 claims to take 'a wide view of the aims and purposes of higher education', but after accepting what it calls the Robbins 'definition', it says nothing about the other three.

The government's view is very simple. The nation's economy needs trained manpower. It is industry that will improve the economy. So we must improve trained manpower for industry. Industry needs scientists and engineers. So let us have more

11

science and engineering students and fewer people studying the arts.

'But why do you want the nation to be more wealthy?', I ask.

'*Don't be silly*', I hear you say, '*Everyone wants more money.*'

'Why?', I insist.

Well, if you've got surplus money after you've bought the necessities of life, you can buy luxuries and entertainment and other things that lead to a happy, contented and enjoyable life.

So what you really want is a happy contented and enjoyable life. Having money is not the only path to happiness and contentment. In fact people with a lot of money are not always the most contented. In any case, if that's what you want, why don't we educate people so that they can be happy, contented and enjoy themselves by other means as well as spending money? For example, most happiness, contentment and enjoyment comes from having good relationships with other people. Shouldn't we educate people about relationships? The social sciences, management and literature all have a role here. In which case it's not only science and engineering that are important. A great deal of enjoyment can also be obtained if we educate people to appreciate the arts, like music. That means we must train people to perform and produce artistic works. So perhaps we should make sure our higher education system trains people in the arts as well as science, engineering and the social sciences.

OK, I accept that we don't only want to train scientists and engineers. Indeed we need doctors, lawyers, teachers and a lot of other professions you haven't mentioned. The question is, 'How many of each?' It's a question of getting the right balance. It ought to be possible to work out how many we need of each and educate the right number.

That's called manpower planning. The government tried it in the 1970s, but it doesn't work except in a very rough and ready way. We know we need more doctors than pharmacists, but we don't know how many. There are a lot of reasons why we can't forecast the numbers needed with acceptable accuracy.

First, it takes many years to train a doctor and quite a few to train a pharmacist, a lawyer, a teacher, an engineer or any other graduate. Courses have to be designed, validated and often accredited by the professions before a college can advertise for applicants. Students begin to apply at least a year before they enter the course. So the time lag between designing a three-year course and students getting jobs having taken it, is likely to be four and a half years at the very least. Now imagine a company trying to forecast its labour requirements for four or five years' time! It's quite impractical.

Second, changing economic conditions affect demand, as do changes in technology.

Third, people do not stay in a job for a lifetime. So we don't know how many graduates we have already trained will move out leaving a vacancy. Furthermore specific job skills do not last a lifetime. But we cannot know for every conceivable skill how long a graduate will retain it. Nor do we know, when a graduate is out of date, whether he will retrain, leave his profession, or do nothing about it.

Fourth, we do not know how many women will return to work in any profession after having children, or how long they will wait to do so. Some return when their children start school. Some return much earlier, some much later and some never at all.

Fifth, we cannot forecast the emigration and immigration for particular professions.

Finally, the assumptions about the traditional age of retirement are no longer valid. In short, although accurate forecasts might be desirable, neither the government, the professional bodies nor the colleges can make useful predictions of the number of graduates who will be needed in any specific profession in four or five years' time.

If planning is no good, we should be able to achieve the right balance of occupational skills by letting free market forces operate. If the country needs more scientists and engineers they will be paid more, and then more schoolchildren will opt to do these subjects.

That doesn't work either. The market that operates is the

more immediate one, the higher education market, not the job market. The country has been short of graduate scientists and engineers for 40 years. Most schoolchildren don't enter higher education because of the money they might get. In one piece of research, students rated 'Interest in my subject' at an average of 3.9 on a scale between 0 and 5. Average ratings for 'Obtaining a general education' and 'Furthering my career' were 3.5 and 3.4 respectively. All other reasons were rated 1.6 or lower.

In any case students' choice of career at this stage is more influenced by what they think they would enjoy doing – that is, expected job satisfaction – than by expectations of high financial rewards. A survey has shown that most school leavers do not have Mrs Thatcher's monetarist values. In any case it is doubtful how effectively information about salaries and job opportunities penetrates the schools.

Furthermore, if the job market was influential, the same time lag problem would apply. The response to demand would only take effect five years later when conditions might have changed. Indeed, most pupils begin to show a preference for arts or science around the age of 13. Most graduates only reach the job market nine years later.

However, I didn't say planning is no good at all; only that manpower planning for specific jobs doesn't work. The less specific the prediction demanded, the more plausible manpower planning becomes. This is partly because, when people change jobs, they are more likely to change to one in the same broad category, than in the same narrow one.

All this means that this aim should be modified to read 'to give instruction in a broad range of occupational skills'. The education should be in general, not specific, occupational skills.

There are educational reasons, too, why we should not always train our graduates for specific jobs. Jobs require specific mental skills based on a combination of sub-skills with much wider application. If you teach the sub-skills separately the job may take longer to learn, but the student will not only do the job better because he will have better understanding of it, but he will also be able to apply the sub-skills to other areas of work.

To keep it simple, let me take an example from everyday life outside the world of higher education. Someone at the cash till of a shop may be taught how to type the cost of each separate purchase into the cash register, press a button to add them up, type in the sum of money proferred, and get the machine to work out the change required. She doesn't need any powers of arithmetic. But if she had some knowledge of arithmetic, she would be able to *understand* what she is doing. She would also be able to answer customers' queries because she would be able to *exercise critical judgement* of whether she has done it correctly. She would not be an automaton pushing buttons. Learning arithmetic would take longer, but it could be *applied* to other areas of her life and could possibly be used in other paid employment.

'Understanding', 'application' and 'exercising critical judgement' are important educational aims of higher education too. They are based upon a knowledge of the principles involved. Principles are generalisations. Much of higher education consists of learning, testing and applying generalisations. Generalisations are necessary in any job where the circumstances for action are not always the same – in other words, where there is complexity. Consider a radiographer. If he tried to learn how to take an X-ray of the wrist, the leg, the chest and so on, all as separate tasks, he would never get to the end of the list; and if he did, he would not do his job very well because every patient is different. He needs to know generalisations about anatomy, radiation physics, etc. and to know how to apply them to a multitude of different cases. Yet even a radiographer's job is simple compared with that of a personnel manager, an accountant, a teacher, or an engineer.

So 'to give instruction in a broad range of occupational skills' is a much more plausible aim for higher education than any aim that is job-specific. This conclusion can be supported by an economic, as well as an educational, argument. Companies are increasingly international. They choose where to build their factories and establish new business. A large potential labour force with a broad base of adaptable occupational skills is a major attraction, if not essential. The nation cannot afford to turn business away by neglecting this aim of higher education.

III. To promote the general powers of the mind

The essence of this aim is the development of the individual. Stand back and look at British universities objectively. They are remarkably successful institutions. Some have lasted 700 years. None has ever closed. All have expanded.

Their influence is enormous. Mankind survives and dominates the environment through the use of knowledge. Universities, and now other institutions of higher education, are the major institutions in our society for the acquisition, preservation, assembly, classification, interrelation, testing, interpretation and dissemination of knowledge, particularly new knowledge. They therefore have a major role in the advancement of our society. They have educated the leaders in politics, administration, the professions and most other walks of life. And, of course, the whole educational system, through which nearly everyone passes, is strongly influenced in its curricula, its examinations, its organisation, its inspectorate and its teachers by ways of thinking disseminated from higher education.

If the influence of higher education is so enormous, this quality is vital. It is not the quantity of knowledge, or of what the knowledge is about, that gives knowledge its quality. It is the way that knowledge is learnt, related, justified and applied that is important. It is the method that matters. It is a matter of attitudes and abilities in thinking. What you think about is less important than your quality of thought.

At one time it was believed that if you get the quality right, you will be able to apply it to anything. You will be a Master of Arts, able to master any art or occupation. I don't think many people would think that now. Nevertheless, the associated belief that what one knows is less important than the quality of one's thinking, that knowledge is less important than intellect, still has a lot of credibility. And employers demonstrate that credibility annually, not only by preferring graduates to non-graduates, but by preferring graduates from institutions with a reputation for training the mind, the intellect, to those knowledgeable in their subject.

That leaves the difficult question of what distinguishes a student with highly educated attitudes and intellect from one who is only well versed in his subject. That was the question tackled by Cardinal Newman in lectures on the founding of Catholic colleges in Ireland in 1852. The resulting book has become a classic. Although almost no one today would think, as he did, that the cultivation of the intellect should be the only aim of a university, few people would deny its importance.

Thus educated, a man will value the truth. He will challenge his roots and rethink the influences of his parents and school. He will exercise judgement that takes years to acquire and will know when judgement should be resisted or withheld. He will be as consistent as possible and aware of his inconsistencies. He will avoid prejudice, discern irrelevance, appreciate implications, restrain his emotions, remove his ignorance and give only due weight to his preoccupations. He will proceed from the known to the unknown and will recognise whereof he cannot speak. (Cf. J. H. Newman, *The Idea of a University*.)

IV. To advance learning

Human beings think they are the most powerful and most important creatures on earth. I sometimes think that whales and certain viruses might also claim this honour. The case in favour of human beings must rest, not only upon the general powers of their mind, but upon their accumulation of knowledge. This is our potential asset and that fact is the reason why we should develop it to the maximum.

If developing knowledge is so important, we should make sure we hang on to what we've got (and that means developing libraries of books, video tapes and computer disks) and we should train people to get new knowledge that is reasonably certain and will stand the test of time. That is the process of doing research and training researchers that takes place in higher education. In many fields, the frontiers of new knowledge are very distant from ordinary people now. That is why training of the best minds is necessary. So training the best minds for research is fundamental to the development of the

17

human race. If we didn't have institutions that did so, it would be necessary to invent them.

There is an objection to that argument. Can industry, the professions and other occupational groups not carry out all the research that is necessary without having special institutions for the job?

There are several answers to this objection. Firstly, it has been estimated that, in cash terms, about 20 per cent of the research done in Britain is indeed done in the private sector. In practice, we don't really know how much is going on, and that is one of the difficulties. If no one else knows about the research that is being carried out, it is hardly making a long-term contribution to the pool of knowledge in books, on tapes and on disks. Academics have an incentive to publish. In industry, competition favours secrecy. Competitors duplicate research.

Second, as remarked in Chapter 1, higher education employs people whose job is not only to keep up to date on the latest knowledge in specialist areas, but also to rub shoulders with people who are up to date in other areas of knowledge so that cross-fertilisation can take place. The private sector rarely has this advantage.

Moreover smaller companies cannot afford to employ permanent full-time researchers. It is much better for them to employ a research organisation when they need it. Universities and polytechnics are such organisations.

Finally, higher education is most important in carrying out fundamental research. This research often seems remote from application yet it is fundamental to other research developments. Yet, because it is fundamental, it is essential to a very wide range of later developments. Essential research that cannot be paid for by the private sector must be paid for by the public purse. It is for this reason Research Councils were established. Tragically, governments have little short-term incentive to encourage the Research Councils to support fundamental research which will not be applied before their next election. With fluctuations in funding, the existence of permanent institutions to maintain the capacity to do fundamental research is important in counteracting the short-term interests of governments.

In short, all these are reasons for having specialist institutions concerned with developing, and exploiting to the maximum, man's major resource – his brain.

V. To develop culture and standards of citizenship

Of the four aims given by the Robbins Committee, this is the most difficult to describe. It is concerned with the ability to see things in different ways and to exercise balanced judgement in the light of those varied perceptions. It is concerned with the ability to see many different sides to a question, to understand different points of view, to appreciate the value of diverse objects and activities, and to understand nations other than our own. This involves having many different concepts which can be used to interpret any situation.

Hence a cultured person is one with breadth of understanding. For this reason, he exhibits tolerance of others who may see things differently. Tolerance is a mark of an educated person. Thus this aim embodies not only skills of perception and judgement, but a number of attitudes. For example the Grimond Report on Birmingham University mentions 'the ability to take responsibility for moral choice' and 'contributing to the educational and general well-being of the community through the application of knowledge and the encouragement of creativity'.

This aim may be criticised as vague sophistry, but some vagueness is inevitable because it emphasises breadth. As soon as concepts like culture and citizenship are made precise, their meaning becomes limited and that is just the opposite of what Robbins wanted to convey.

This aim can also be misunderstood in two other ways. One is that the cultured person is someone who appreciates certain kinds of art, engages in certain leisure activities and who can communicate effectively. It is too often forgotten that science is a major aspect of our culture. The idea that science students need a dollop of humanities in order to be cultured, but that humanities students don't need to know any science is a travesty of higher education. Social skills are also part of our culture. This aim was important for Robbins because he was particularly critical of the early specialisation and over-specialisation in our educational system. In this respect, Scottish schooling was preferred to that in England and Wales.

The preservation of democracy is another important aspect of this aim. Because we take it for granted, we often forget it; and I hope you will forgive me when I give reminders. Democracy is part of our culture. It increasingly assumes that people can make sophisticated judgements and that research is available for them to do so. Judgement and research are the stuff of higher education.

VI. Aims from other perspectives

If you look again at the first paragraph of the last section, you will see it is about exploring a question from many different perspectives. That is just what we've been doing in this chapter. Section I on attitudes and emotions is particularly from a parent's perspective although employers and many others are also concerned about the attitudes of new graduates. Section II is more from the perspective of the government. Section III is more concerned with developing the individual. Section IV is about the accumulation of knowledge, experience and wisdom for posterity; while the perspective of Section V is about the community in which graduates will live and work. It has a social perspective.

These perspectives don't usually conflict, but they could do. There are also many other perspectives that could be taken. Some of them are a mixture of the five perspectives already taken. For example I could take a financial perspective that higher education is an investment in people. Particularly when there are going to be fewer people of working age, those we have should be educated to increase productivity per working person. This seems like a mixture of Sections II and III.

Another perspective is administrative: higher education provides experts. The experts may be consultants or critics. As consultants academics are used by the government, the Civil Service, industry and commerce. As critics, academic work may be viewed from a constitutional perspective. Academic work can also be seen from the standpoint of its effect upon the environment, upon world health and poverty and upon international relations. Researchers can be seen as an international community with common interests and values. Higher education is an agent of change; and this is another perspective. No doubt there are many more perspectives that could be added.

The important point is that no single perspective should exclude the others. Diversity is desirable in higher education. It produces a creative tension because each perspective emphasises some values more than others. Single-mindedness is inimical to higher education. For this reason its values, and hence its whole style of organisation, is quite different from many undertakings in industry and commerce.

Chapter 3

HOW THE SYSTEM DEVELOPED

The principles of higher education come from ancient Athens

Western civilisation has evolved from three earlier cultures. From Galilee it obtained its religion, many of its moral principles, its national and domestic rituals, its community focus, the stability of the family and its softer values including its service to those it loves, its care for those that suffer, its compassion for the weak and its concern for the needy. From Rome it inherited the basis of its laws, the foundations of its government, its separation of judiciary and executive, the rigour of its organisation, its repression of human feelings and its use of military power. From Athens it acquired its desire for knowledge, its scientific quest, its pursuit of arts and its canons of criticism.

Their legacies in Britain are represented by the Church, the State and the universities. Yet each is concerned with the affairs of the others. None has been exclusively concerned with the power of the spirit, the power of government or the powers of the mind. Nor has any exclusively valued the soul, material wealth or ideas. Yet each has had some constitutional independence. Consequently they exist in a mutual tension, each keeping the excesses of the others in check. In different phases of history one has dominated the others or a coalition has prevailed upon the third. It is easy to think of the Middle Ages as when the Church had more temporal and educational power than today; while in the past ten years the government has increasingly obliged the universities to serve its will.

It may seem harder to think of a time when the universities dominated the Church and State; but that is because we tend to think of power in terms of political, administrative, legal or military power – the values of Rome, not the values of

Athens. The powers of the mind are altogether more indirect and general. The effects of education are not immediate, but they last a lifetime and pervade everything a person does. That is power indeed.

What is important in the legacy from Athens is not an institution. (The first universities, as we know them, were not established at Bologna and Paris until the twelfth century, nearly 1,800 years later.) Nor was the legacy a body of knowledge. (What is regarded as certain knowledge in one period, is often shown to be mistaken or meaningless in another.)

The important legacy is the method of advancing knowledge. Instead of propounding his beliefs, Socrates asked questions. In his case they were usually philosophical questions, such as what we mean by justice, friendship or reality; but the subject matter is irrelevant. Socrates's method was to probe the answers given with more questions, thereby taking his students ever deeper into the subject. He often showed that their common-sense beliefs were inconsistent, or conflicted, with other evidence. While his students learnt about the subject, they also learnt what they did not, and could not, know. They learnt about themselves.

This method is still central to university teaching and research today, and it brings the two together as part of the same activity – the quest for understanding by criticism of ideas. It has the following crucial features. A recognition that:

- no belief is so sacred that it cannot be challenged;
- knowledge is tentative, not fixed and static. It is constantly being discarded or reshaped, created or reinvented, discovered and expanded;
- learning is a research activity, a voyage of discovery;
- the voyage progresses by ideas being subjected to critical tests, in particular, common observation and the impartiality of reason, not the authority of individuals or organisations, whatever their position or wealth;
- discussion is an essential process – asking and anticipating questions, penetrating questions, is an essential skill;

- the most effective teaching consists of pulling ideas out of students, not drumming them in; and
- there should not only be tolerance of those who hold opinions that threaten one's own, but active co-operation in assisting them to pursue the truth wherever it may lead.

The process of questioning includes challenging the answers given by authorities, whether those authorities be the government, the Church, teachers, experts, those with experience, employers or parents. If you cannot understand this questioning attitude, you cannot understand what distinguishes higher education from other areas of learning. The persistent challenging of those with authority creates a tension in our society that is innovative and constantly adapting to change. Without that constant challenge, our society will be static, out of date, backward and miserable. That is why 'Britain needs its universities', why students ought to be radical – that is, to rethink the fundamentals of everything, and why they are at a time of life when some rebellion is to be understood and encouraged.

Athens produced Aristotle, probably the greatest intellect who ever lived. He is thought to have written over 400 volumes. His work on logic stood unrivalled until just over 100 years ago. His books on ethics and metaphysics are still studied today. He also wrote, albeit less convincingly to modern eyes, on astronomy, physics, mathematics, geology, politics, marriage, education, psychology and art. Many of the basic concepts of science came from his mind. He was tutor to Alexander the Great. Above all, he was a naturalist. Species are still being rediscovered that he had dissected and described. (You may think he did all this without a research grant. You would be wrong! Alexander's soldiers brought back specimens and documents galore. Someone has estimated that the cost would be the equivalent of over £200 million in modern currency.)

Medieval knowledge came from authorities and contested discussion

Yet in a way, the forerunners of the medieval university, Plato's 'Academy' and Aristotle's 'Lyceum', were almost too successful. For a very long time afterwards, ordinary mortals felt there was no point in going on a journey of discovery themselves. If they wanted to find the truth about something, it was usually easier to look up what Aristotle or other ancient scholars had said about it. The classical writers had become authorities.

The question for medieval scholars was how to interpret what the ancients said, rather than replicate their findings. Indeed, replication of many classical observations would have been impossible in England. The sky, plants, animals, politics, religion and social behaviour were different in Greece.

The lecture system developed because not everyone could look up what the ancients said for themselves. There were too few manuscripts and not everyone could read classical Latin and Greek. A lecture was something literally read from a 'lectern'.

Discussion was still the central process to resolve disagreements, but the technique of disputation was more commonly used. As in our parliament and our law courts, this tended to be a two-sided contest rather than one displaying a diversity of possible opinions. It had one interesting technique which would be good for students to use occasionally today: before replying to an opponent, they were expected to summarise his argument. This not only encouraged accurate listening and understanding, but it also produced more appreciation of the merits of the opponent's case.

We should not undervalue the medieval scholars, but their reliance upon the authority of the classics, the Church and the State runs contrary to our modern emphasis upon encouraging students to observe and think for themselves. There is a story that several monks were considering the question of how many teeth a horse has. They looked at all the documents and sources of reference they could lay their hands on and debated long and hard all day and well into the night. With this question still unresolved and when it was getting very late, one young monk ventured to ask if he might be allowed to speak. On permission being granted, he suggested that right now they should take a lantern, go down to the stables, open the mouth of the horse, count its teeth and settle the matter.

Whereupon the elders turned upon him, and chastised his impudence for supposing that his own observations could outweigh the opinions of all the scholars that had ever preceded him.

This subservience should warn ordinary citizens that society will stagnate if higher education is allowed to be dominated by the wealthy, the Church or the State.

In Britain it was not until the Renaissance, the Reformation and the scientific revolution that followed, that the mould of medieval thought began to be broken, and even then, it was not broken by the universities. Yet those changes are part of the heritage of higher education.

The growing freedoms of expression, opinion, observation and criticism

The fifteenth, sixteenth and seventeenth centuries slowly established hard-won liberties that constantly have to be defended. First, there was a new-found freedom of expression in the arts, particularly in Italy (the Italian Renaissance) and Elizabethan England. But the resistance of the Church meant that the study of arts stayed mostly outside the universities. Painting, musical performance, sport, sculpture, dance and ballet, to name but a few, remained largely outside the higher education system until very recently. Yet without the free expression of imagination and feelings, there cannot be a genuine search for truths, values and ideas. Without that search, education will not be *higher* education. It is a freedom that tutors in arts and humanities today try to release in their students, often to undo the conformity of schools.

Second, there was a humanist movement. It was an intellectual movement, initially preaching tolerance, ridiculing the hypocrisy of the Church and reinterpreting the Athenian legacy with the aid of new documents and scholars arriving from Greece after the fall of Constantinople in 1453. Its importance for higher education today lies in a new confidence in humanity – that people can learn things for themselves and exercise their own judgement. This confidence is something higher education constantly strives to give its students. In short, Renaissance humanism gave a new value to the individual – his beliefs, his rights and his feelings. Without it, the Reformation – the breaking away of the Church of England and the Lutheran Church from the Church of Rome – would not have been possible. Equally, although men and women continued for some time to be persecuted for their beliefs, the break-aways gave a political freedom that in turn reinforced the greater value placed on the individual.

Individualism permits original thinking. Originality is the first step to human advancement and is the essence of research. That is why human advancement and higher education go together. The greater value and confidence in the individual naturally led to more trust in his powers of observation as a way of gaining knowledge. That is fundamental to modern science.

So, third, the dormant seeds of scientific thought sown in Athens 1,800 years before, were germinated. To quote Bertrand Russell's *History of Western Philosophy*:

> It is not what the man of science believes that distinguishes him, but how and why he believes it. His beliefs are tentative, not dogmatic. They are based upon evidence, not upon intuition or authority. The founders of modern science showed great patience in observation and great boldness in forming their hypotheses. The authority of science is intellectual, not governmental. No penalties befall those who reject it; acceptance is not motivated by prudence. It prevails by its intrinsic appeal to reason. It is moreover, a piece-meal and partial authority. It does not, like Catholic dogma, lay down a complete system covering human morality, the past and future history of the universe.

The tentativeness of the academic integrity produces a temper of mind very different from the dogmas of a Prime Minister or the Church.

These three things are concerned with the right to express one's opinions and feelings openly, the value of individual human beings and the pursuit of the truth. No doubt they are not absolutes, but they are values fundamental to higher education.

They are values that were contrary to those of the Church at that time and that fact has had a profound effect upon curricula in schools and colleges ever since. The values of the Church were based upon discipline not free expression, faith not doubt, corporate wisdom not individualism, and bookish learning not scientific observation.

The struggle to establish science, technology and practical subjects

There have been three divisions in higher education curricula which have been slow to heal: arts/science, theory/practice and memory/thinking. Scars remain because the cuts were deep.

A period of decadence

Science seemed to conflict with religion. In England, the Church effectively controlled the schools and the universities by its system of endowments and it did not encourage the study of science. Admission to Oxford and Cambridge was not possible without religious tests until after 1854. Little science or engineering, except mathematics and medicine, was taught until after the Devonshire Commission of 1872.

Because of curricular control by the Church, throughout the sixteenth, seventeenth and eighteenth centuries the universities were in decline. The most important intellectual and cultural advances were made outside higher education. True, Sir Thomas More the political theorist, Harvey the physician, Hobbes and Locke the philosophers, and Sir Isaac Newton the astronomer and mathematician all went to a university; and that may have strengthened the mythical belief that a classical education fits you for anything. But they did not do their significant work there. Others, not least Shakespeare and Sir Francis Bacon, never went to university at all. The same might be said about Michelangelo, Leonardo, Galileo, Pascal and others on the continent of Europe.

In England the greatest interest in science, inventions, discoveries and new ideas was in clubs and societies meeting in most of the major cities, not in the two universities of Oxford and Cambridge. For example, the Royal Society was founded in 1660, societies for literature and architecture in the 1730s, the British Museum in 1753, the Royal Society of Arts, Manufacturing and Commerce in 1754, the Royal Institution in 1799 and the British Association for the Advancement of Science in 1831.

Notice that although the two universities in England were mostly attended by young gentlemen who might spend a life of leisure, science too, was a leisure pursuit for the wealthy. Working men who wanted to study science in an applied way went to the Mechanics' Institutes and Working Men's Clubs which were opening in the evenings in many cities.

The universities taught bookish subjects more for memory than creative imagination. Very often the aim was to be able to recall encyclopaedic facts like people on *Mastermind* or other modern quiz shows. In France these scholars were called 'Encyclopedists'. Arts such as painting, architecture, music, agriculture, navigation, dance, acting, government, engineering and many others were not only not taught, their practitioners were often regarded as inferior people. Practical and manual skills were given low status.

These prejudices are still with us. They are socially divisive, educationally narrow and conceptually mistaken. Professions and organisations which wanted to improve their educational standards, set up their own colleges outside the universities. That is why specialist professional colleges in agriculture, music, art, technology and paramedical subjects, were at first outside the education system. By the 1850s there were over 50 teacher training colleges, almost all supported by religious foundations.

So the fragmentation of higher education provision has deep historical roots based upon bookish learning and attitudes about what is academically respectable. Only in the last twenty years has reintegration within a higher education system made significant progress. Even now, vested and political interests, assumptions about subject boundaries, prejudices about combining practical and theoretical skills, preconceptions about other people's occupations and professions, and traditions of organisation and finance too often get in the way.

The nineteenth-century revival

It was only with the coming of the Industrial Revolution that the joint pressure of scientists, the London medical schools,

Catholics, nonconformists, liberals, free thinkers and others successfully demanded a university that would teach beyond the Oxbridge curriculum. University College, London, was founded by Jeremy Bentham in 1827 on condition that no religion was taught in it. He believed education should be directly useful. Like the four Scottish universities it taught law, economics, medicine, mathematics, chemistry, modern languages and moral philosophy as well as the classics. It was non-residential. Its exams were taken by working- and middle-class men studying at home and at colleges such as the Mechanics' Institutes and Working Men's Colleges. By 1849 it also admitted women, although women were not awarded degrees until 1878.

Thus a second tradition of British higher education became established. On the one hand, Oxbridge was aristocratic, clerical, elitist, concentrating on a liberal education in arts and humanities, and providing mainly non-vocational courses. Its staff and students were well connected with people in national positions of power and providing 70 per cent of the Civil Service. On the other hand, in the second half of the nineteenth century several of the industrial cities, such as Manchester, Birmingham, Leeds and Sheffield, established civic universities which were locally supported, vocationally orientated, and closely related to, and dependent upon, local business and industry, with middle-class students largely living at home.

These two traditions represent a conflict that still exists between the ideals of a general liberal education and a vocational education. Today many people will see universities as representing the traditional liberal values, while the polytechnics and other colleges in the public sector have vocational ideals. But that is a mistake. The conflict is in our minds, not between institutions. All institutions embody both ideals.

I may have made the same mistake. I have portrayed the growth of science, technology and vocational education as if it was a process of overcoming the clerical and aristocratic preconceptions of otherworldly academics in ivory towers at Oxbridge. There was some truth in that before the nineteenth century; but the preconception was even stronger in the worlds of commerce, business and industry. Even in the 1950s many employers hesitated to take on science and engineering graduates because they thought them too theoretical.

That conflict reached its peak in the middle of the nineteenth century. It is hard to realise now, that education was still seen by many people as the prerogative of the Church or other religious organisations, not the State or the individual. The greatest advocate of this viewpoint in higher education was Cardinal Newman, whose opinions I dealt with in Chapter 2. More than his predecessors in the liberal tradition, Newman emphasised intellectual thought, not encyclopaedic memory. Newman believed the first step in intellectual training is to learn to apply a system of rules. That is why a schoolboy's education (the education of girls does not seem to enter Newman's scheme of things) should begin with grammar and then mathematics. The grammar is the grammar of Latin and Greek.

Newman's view of learning had a strong influence on school curricula because headmasters saw universities as the path to success. The idea that 'Grammar' schools were for the most intelligent who aspire to higher education, technical schools for those with practical skills, and senior schools for unskilled workers, persisted until the Education Act of 1944. White-collar workers have long been seen as superior to engineers or those who make things and do manual or physical work. As late as 1960, Advanced-level Latin or Greek was a necessary entry qualification for undergraduates seeking arts degrees at London University. Only very recently have employment-based skills begun to find a place in educational curricula. 'Education' has been conceived as academic, while 'training' has been seen as more practical and vocationally relevant. Even to this day the fee-paying schools send more students to university to study arts subjects, while State comprehensive schools send more undergraduates to study science.

Science is an activity. It is a process of discovery. It is more concerned with experiment than studying books. It involves research more than scholarship. Thus it was that the growth of science in higher education also meant the growing recognition of research as a service offered by civic universities to local industry and governments. This linkage of science and

31

research came from Germany which was a growing scientific and military power in the late nineteenth and early twentieth centuries. It is small wonder that British governments took fright and said 'we must have scientific and military research too' and the universities increasingly said 'OK, but you must pay for it'. They both still do.

Government responsibility for finance and the 'buffer principle'

There has been a growing demand for student places throughout the nineteenth and twentieth centuries. Higher education has been seen as the path to success. In addition, as I have just said, from the 1850s professors were increasingly expected to do research. These two factors placed a strain upon university resources. From 1889 onwards the government helped universities financially from time to time. At the end of the First World War there were a large number of returning heroes who wanted to go to university.

Accordingly, in 1919, the Treasury authorised a University Grants Committee (UGC) 'To enquire into the financial needs of university education in Great Britain; and to advise the Government as to the application of any grants that may be made by Parliament towards meeting them'. The Committee, established almost casually, continued for 70 formative years until it was replaced by the Universities Funding Council in 1989. (See p. 47.)

By its formation the government tacitly recognised that the provision of higher education is a matter of national concern, not merely a private matter. And it recognised its responsibility to maintain it. Even more important, a 'buffer' was created between the government and the universities (the buffer principle). That is, the government of the day acknowledged the freedom of the universities to manage their own affairs without interference, even though they were partly funded by government. That was less an academic freedom for individuals; more a managerial freedom for institutions.

Many people, particularly those from abroad, find the buffer principle difficult to understand. Perhaps an analogy is the best way to explain this freedom. The government pays the salary of the Leader of the Opposition in Parliament because it is recognised that good government requires an effective and respected opposition. The opposition should expose incompetence by effectively publicising the truth. It is also the job of higher education to seek and publicise the truth. That includes truths that may either support or oppose the government view. The assumption that higher education exists purely for the sake of those engaged in it (who should therefore bear its total cost) is wholly misleading. It has an important role in the preservation of democracy and good government that is worth paying for. That is why the government has a responsibility to pay for it. The reason is constitutional.

At first the proportion of university income from government grants was small. Over the years it has increased not only because the number of students has increased, new buildings have been required and new universities have been established, but because the nation has required a great deal of research. Government support of both teaching and research is known as 'the dual funding system'.

In financing university research, governments have also recognised that they have a special responsibility to fund universities for financial and strategic reasons. Much of the research has been fundamental, such as research into the nature of the atom. This research was not of immediate use to industry, but was invaluable later (e.g. for the nuclear power industry). Naturally it is part of the nature of research that you don't always know what you are going to find out. If you did, there would often be no point in doing it. By financing fundamental research, the government recognised that it has a responsibility to risk funding research with uncertain or long delayed benefits and high set-up costs. No one in the commercial world could reasonably take such long-term and costly risks.

1964–72 was a period of accelerated expansion

The year 1964 is a crucial date in the development of British higher education as we now know it. The Robbins Report on Higher Education was accepted by the incoming Labour government. The steeply rising birth rate peaked in that year, then fell just as steeply until 1978. The widespread introduction of contraceptives and the legalising of abortion meant that by 1978 only two children were born for every three in 1964. The Robbins Report was probably the most thoroughly researched government report of all time – a fitting tribute to its subject.

The Robbins Committee said that 'courses of higher education should be available for all those who are qualified by ability and attainment to pursue them and who wish to do so'. This is often known as the 'Robbins principle'. They added a proviso that is often forgotten: that, for educational and vocational reasons, broader courses for the first degree should be taken by a much greater number of students.

They justified the principle, first on the grounds that a nation's economic growth and higher cultural standards can only be achieved by making the most of the talents of its citizens. And second, because 'the good society desires equality of opportunity for its citizens to become not merely good producers but also good men and women'. In the modern context, what is significant about these two reasons is that higher education for a few is justified in terms of the common good, not merely for the benefit of the individuals who receive it. Higher education is justified not in terms of competition and the selfish aspirations of those gifted enough to take advantage of it, but in terms of the contribution that those individuals can make to the welfare of us all.

The Robbins principle implied a big expansion of higher education. The Committee believed that demand for full-time higher education would rise from 216,000 in 1962/63 to 390,000 in 1973/74 and 560,000 in 1980/81. The Committee not only wanted more, broader courses, but less early specialisation and more students taking more than one main subject. They recommended regular course reviews to reduce overloading.

With what they believed to be a continually rising birth rate, the Committee felt that the number and status of teachers in training should be increased. The teacher training colleges were to be called Colleges of Education. The professional training, then recently extended to three years, and now a fourth year, could be added for an increasing number of teachers to obtain the degree of Bachelor of Education (BEd). Groups of colleges of education were to be federated under an Institute of Education within a university and to submit their degrees for the approval of university senates. Suitable students were to be able to transfer to university Honours courses in midstream. Local education authorities were to be represented on the governing bodies of colleges of education. The Institutes of Education and the University Departments of Education were to form Schools of Education on whose governing bodies there should be assessors appointed by the Minister of Education.

I have described how the historical reluctance of universities to teach science, technology and vocational disciplines resulted in specialist Colleges of Technology, Art, Agriculture, Music and other disciplines. Successive governments had wanted to encourage science and technology at higher levels and the Robbins Committee recommended that several Colleges of Advanced Technology (CATs) and Central Institutions (CIs) in Scotland should be given university status. A number of institutions, such as the colleges of Science and Technology at Manchester and Glasgow, should be selected for rapid development. The Royal College of Art and the College of Aeronautics should come under the ambit of the University Grants Committee. Universities were encouraged to form links with government research establishments and industry. The Committee envisaged a hierarchy of regional, area and local colleges without university status. These colleges were also encouraged to develop a wider range of advanced full-time courses to be validated in future by a Council for National Academic Awards (CNAA) which would cover the whole of Great Britain, would be established under a Royal Charter and should establish degree standards equivalent to those of the universities.

Universities were to provide 350,000 of the 560,000 places needed in 1980/81. Six new universities should be established, many existing ones should be expanded to 8,000 or 10,000 places and there should be 145,000 places for intending teachers in colleges of education. These colleges should include training for other professions, either by diversifying their courses or by merging with other institutions.

How to get out of an impossible commitment – centralise control

The commitment

Although both the major political parties accepted the Robbins Report at the time, its recommendations have posed a problem for governments ever since. Acceptance of the Robbins Principle implied increasing government expenditure for the foreseeable future. Acceptance of the buffer principle implied no government control over how the money was spent.

No government can tolerate that situation for long. It was an impossible commitment that would go on for ever. New universities, new buildings, more staff and more facilities involved increasing capital and recurrent expenditure by central government. New and expanding regional, area and local colleges involved new expenditure by local government; and the commitment of local government to supply apparently ever-growing numbers of students with grants involved expenditure over which they, too, had no control.

The Robbins Committee was well aware of both the expenditure and the independence of universities. They had visited many other countries where governments exerted stronger controls upon higher education, and returned convinced that the British system was better. Indeed, the British system has been the envy of the world and its freedom has contributed to its prestige. That prestige has brought financial and political dividends because it has placed Britain among the world leaders in scientific, commercial and educational projects.

How to increase control

The history of higher education since 1964 has been a story of the government trying to reduce its financial commitment and increase its control. In terms of the three cultures with which I began this chapter, it has been a period of reasserting the values of Rome – the power of government. Care for the individual (the heritage of Galilee) and fundamental research (the Athenian quest) flowered in the immediate post-Robbins years, but have increasingly succumbed in the 1980s.

Using a different framework of thinking, control of higher education can always be conceived as a triangular tension between the providers (the universities, polytechnics, colleges and their staffs), its customers (employers and students) and central agencies (e.g. government departments, the CNAA, the professional bodies such as the British Medical Association and the Institution of Civil Engineers). The mechanisms of control are of two kinds: academic and financial. Universities had jealously guarded their academic autonomy and academic standards but the new CNAA was a central validating body. The Robbins proposals swung control towards the providers and student applicants as customers. Since then the government has been trying to move control back to central agencies and give more to employers as customers.

Establish the 'binary system'

In 1967, in a speech at Woolwich, Anthony Crosland, the Minister of Education, announced that 30 new institutions called polytechnics would be established by upgrading and merging existing institutions. Polytechnic courses were to be academically validated by the CNAA, not by universities. They would be financed by local government contributing to a central pool from which central government would allocate the funds. Compared with universities, polytechnics were to provide more occupationally related courses, to be more concerned with teaching than research and to be more locally based. This implied more home-based students, more ties with industry and commerce, and a greater variety of full-time, part-time, sandwich, 'evenings only' and short-term courses. The balance between arts and science courses should be strongly weighted to science and technology.

Crosland thereby established the 'binary system' in which there are independent universities on the one hand and a range of institutions under some form of governmental control on the other. Under a binary policy, an institution is one side or the other of a line dividing the private and public sectors. The alternative policy, which has often been discussed, is to have no sharp dividing line but a 'seamless robe' in which there is a range of institutions whose characteristics form a continuum.

Use public reaction to student protest

In 1968, there were worldwide student protests seeking more representation in university and college affairs, and more occupational relevance in their courses. Many of the students were left-wing and the long-term damage to the image and reputation of students, and higher education as a whole, has been profound. It strengthened an erroneous impression that students are undisciplined, ungrateful, ill-kempt layabouts. It created public and political disenchantment with higher education which was not there four years before. And it generated a reaction and a Conservative resolve to be tough.

Seek friendly co-operation

In 1969, Shirley Williams, then Minister for Higher Education, asked universities to consider a number of reforms that would reduce costs. These included the reduction of student grants, substituting loans, requiring students to undertake specified employment for a period after graduation, and requiring more students to be resident at home. The style was consultative. The Vice-Chancellors were not very receptive.

Make sure the DES keeps control of the OU

In 1970, the Open University, originally called the University of the Air, opened for part-time, home-based adults. It was directly financed by the Department of Education and Science (DES), not the University Grants Committee, thus ensuring some government influence. It uncovered an unsuspected demand for continuing education and the cost of each graduate was only one-quarter of the cost in a traditional university. In the light of that fact, governments have tried to encourage distance learning methods when appropriate ever since. But, because they minimise interpersonal interaction, they are not appropriate for the social and emotional aims of education, nor the deepest levels of criticism (see Chapter 2).

Abandon the quinquennial system

In 1975, the government further increased its short-term influence on university finance by abandoning the quinquennial system in which funding was based on a five-year programme.

Pull the colleges of education into the public sector

In response to government pressure, the colleges of education heroically expanded both their output of teachers and the length of their courses in the 1960s. Developments in psychology and sociology and the publication of government reports on primary and secondary education stimulated them to recast their courses and to develop a new breed of teachers. These teachers were more understanding of children's cognitive development and their social and emotional needs, and were able to use new methods of teaching effectively. The colleges of education were staffed by men and women totally dedicated, but lacking political clout.

In the 1970s, owing to the demographic drop and their inability as monotechnic institutions to diversify their professional courses, over half the colleges were closed. Others were pulled, struggling and screaming, into the public sector. Some were merged. Some were absorbed by polytechnics. For most of them, their connection with university institutes was unwillingly broken and their courses were validated by the CNAA. The colleges felt betrayed. The teaching profession felt undervalued. Morale was deflated. Lecturers retired in droves.

Get full cost fees from overseas students

In 1977, the government insisted that students from overseas should not be subsidised by the British taxpayer. Superficially this action seemed fair and a way of saving some money. In practice, the students went elsewhere, income was lost and great damage was done to Commonwealth and international relations. It showed, once again, that governments who think of higher education purely in terms of a vocational training fail to understand its contribution to human relations, both at home and abroad.

Use finance to promote occupationally related courses

The Robbins Committee believed that universities would respond to the challenge of producing more innovative and occupationally related courses. In the event, while some universities attempted innovations, most expansion was 'more of the same'. There was a swing away from science and vocationally orientated courses among applicants from schools. In the competition for expansion, universities were loath to turn away students in the arts and humanities by offering science and engineering places that could not be filled. There was another reason for the expansion of arts and humanities. They were cheaper to produce. A graduate in science and technology cost two or three times, and a doctor six times, as much.

The polytechnics had been established partly because the government was disappointed at the universities' failure to produce more students from occupationally related courses. By the end of the 1970s, it was clear that the polytechnics too had expanded far more in arts and humanities than in science, technology and courses directly related to jobs.

In 1979, the Manpower Services Commission (MSC) and all its youth training schemes, were placed under the Department of Employment. The Minister of Education failed to convince the Cabinet that it should be under the Department of Education and Science (DES). The DES was perceived as unable to make post-secondary education more occupationally related. Two years later, the Open Tech, an attempt to form a technological counterpart to the Open University, was placed under the Manpower Services Commission.

Background to the cuts

Previous governments this century had used many academics as advisers. The Thatcher government used more industrialists and financiers. Naturally their values were overwhelmingly financial. A simplistic impression was given that industrialists produced wealth while education and social services consumed it; and that education was not producing graduates with the right employable skills. The false assumptions behind such smears could not be exposed quickly in the pressures of television debate and it was soon clear that cutting higher education would not lose many votes. (Nor can the smears be rebuffed without excessive digression here. Suffice to ask the reader to consider how efficient industry would be without graduates contributing to the good health, social welfare and personal well-being of working people and their families. Industry, commerce, education, health and social services interact. They cannot validly be seen in financial isolation; still less in competition. The relationship between education and the economy is not a direct one. Moreover it could be retorted that British research and inventiveness has a high reputation; but that British industry has not always capitalised on it. Furthermore industrialists continued to value arts graduates with those supposedly unemployable skills by avidly employing them.)

The previous paragraph reflects a feeling of 'us and them' that was created between higher education and industry in the early 1980s. High inflation had hit industries in the 1970s while employers saw higher education as expanding with government money. In reality, universities were cut back too. From 1973 onwards until the end of the decade the funding to produce a graduate virtually halved in real terms. It was in fact a period of increasing efficiency. But it did not seem so. Because inflation was high and student numbers were rising steeply, costs were rising. So the money spent looked like a sharp increase.

The public sector was not cut in the same way. During the 1970s the polytechnics expanded, developed their own individuality and matured. The reputation of the CNAA had grown. Many local authorities viewed their polytechnics with justifiable pride and encouraged the diversity of courses for which they were established.

Their encouragement is not surprising. They got more than they paid for. Because local authorities without a polytechnic also contributed to the pool of funds, there was a net flow of cash to those local authorities that had one. Furthermore, the Robbins principle imposed no limit to the expansion, provided there were sufficient students able and willing to pursue the courses.

With its policy to cut local government expenditure and take more central control, the Thatcher government soon (1980) stopped the expansion by limiting the size of the pool of local government money that could be used by polytechnics; and in 1982 it set up a National Advisory Body for Local Authority Higher Education (NAB) to allocate the money according to what courses should be encouraged in the national interest.

The 1981 cuts

In 1981, the government was ideologically committed to cutting public expenditure. Institutions starved of finance are more compliant than ones which are well supplied. With the expected fall in the number of 18 to 20 year-olds from 1983 onwards, higher education was an obvious target. Funding to the universities and the public sector institutions was cut by nearly 20 per cent. Furthermore, tuition fees were halved, not to help those students who paid their own fees, but to remove the incentive for institutions to replace their income by recruiting more students. (So much for freedom and enterprise. When they conflicted, control by the government was more important.)

The irony of this policy, which the government had not foreseen, was to savage those universities with an emphasis upon science, technology and other vocational courses. Why? The only way to make savings was to cut staff. The salaries of academic staff account for half the costs of a university or polytechnic. The salaries of other staff account for another quarter. Therefore the only way to make savings approaching 20 per cent was to cut staff, particularly academic staff. But academic staff in universities had tenure. They could not be made redundant. Therefore there had to be a system of early retirements. But to make young staff retire would be very expensive, not only because their pension would have to be paid for many years to come, but because their pension fund would suddenly have to be increased by lump payments by the UGC or directly by central government. The younger staff who could not be retired were those who were recruited during the rapid expansion of the late 1960s and early 1970s. But owing to the swing against science, these staff were particularly in arts and humanities. On the other hand, staff in the former

Colleges of Advanced Technology (ex-CATs) were typically recruited to teaching in the late 1950s after ten years' industrial experience. They were much older. They could be pensioned off at much less expense. Thus it was that the institutions to suffer most severely were the universities of Salford, Aston and Bradford, in other words, technological universities situated in the conurbations of Manchester, Birmingham and West Yorkshire, not the arts universities of the south and east.

By 1982 the Robbins Principle was dying. In effect the government had renounced its commitment. Student numbers were constrained. Qualified applicants could not gain admittance. As a buffer the UGC now seemed thin and the NAB was beginning to constrain provision in the public sector. Government influence was significantly increased.

Shaping the Education Reform Act 1988

Having increased its power, the government had to decide what to do with it. Industrialists believed higher education was poorly managed and if only higher education was organised like industry, it would be less expensive and more efficient.

Increasing managerial influence

Spurred by criticisms and the threat of a government enquiry, in 1984 Vice-Chancellors and Principals set up their own Committee (CVCP) under the chairmanship of Sir Alex Jarratt, a prominent industrialist, to study the 'efficiency' of universities. Universities were found to be well managed, but the Committee itself overspent its budget! The concept of 'efficiency' is inappropriate to some aspects of university work. 'Efficiency' is concerned with the costs to achieve predetermined objectives. But research and the best forms of teaching are adventures of discovery. There cannot be predetermined objectives without already having discovered what you set out to discover. Perhaps for this reason, the Committee was solely concerned with the management of universities, not its academic or educational policies, practices and methods.

The Jarratt Committee made some useful recommendations

43

to the government, the University Grants Committee (UGC), the CVCP itself and to universities in general. It proposed that the government should facilitate long-term planning in universities by suggesting broad policy guidelines and restoring a longer-term funding horizon as there used to be with the quinquennial system. It recommended a review of the role of the UGC and wanted to encourage it to collaborate more closely with universities by making its views known and increasing discussion of them. It suggested that a range of performance indicators should be developed to enable comparisons between universities and that the CVCP should extend its training of senior university personnel. It advised universities to have rolling academic and institutional plans, more budget delegation in a hierarchy of cost centres, and more staff development, appraisal and accountability in the light of these plans and delegated financial responsibilities.

These recommendations have had a considerable effect. The UGC made financial incentives for their implementation and the Vice-Chancellors could hardly ignore a report they themselves had commissioned. The devolution of financial responsibility to cost centres roughly corresponding to academic departments, created much more financial awareness and economy among staff below head of department level. For twenty years, staff training and development activities had been ignored, if not resisted by many staff. With the introduction of appraisal schemes and more confident support by Vice-Chancellors, they have become more widely recognised and acceptable.

In 1985, the government asked the NAB to carry out a similar review of public sector management. It worked in a similar way carrying out case studies in four polytechnics, two colleges of higher education, two voluntary colleges and two colleges with a mixture of further education and advanced further education. Likewise, they split the task into four topics: management, institutional functioning, the use of resources and marketing. Many of the recommendations were similar too. On finance, they wanted the government to give longer-term policy horizons and much greater freedom to manage their budgets within a given sum. They proposed that governing bodies should have up to one-third of their members from the local education authorities, but the institutions should be allowed to pursue their own personnel policies. There was to be increased public accountability with all institutions providing statements of their objectives and how far they were achieved in an annual report, which should also include the statement of audited accounts. Most of these recommendations are implicit in the Education Reform Act 1988.

What is left to control?

So how was the government progressing in taking control? It had brought expenditure under control. Now the Jarratt and NAB reports could justify legislation for controlling managerial style and removing the power of local authorities. But it did not have academic control. If it could get rid of the UGC and the buffer principle, it could substitute another body to increase control of what subjects are researched, taught and learnt (the UFC). A similar body could do the same for the public sector (the PCFC). (See p. 47.)

Financial incentives

The government could also persuade institutions to do what it wanted by financial incentives. Institutions starved of finance may be tempted to do the government's bidding for a morsel of money. Incentives, it may be argued, do not infringe freedom. But they may pose a moral dilemma for some institutions. The interests of the truth and of education are not well served if only those with money can offer incentives. (For example, the needs of the poor might be less well researched than the needs of business.) Higher education must always be vigilant against indoctrination and bribery.

In 1987 the Manpower Services Commission (now the Training Agency) offered a million pounds over five years to institutions incorporating experience in an economic environment into degree programmes for virtually all their students. The scheme is called Enterprise in Higher Education. Such experience is not necessarily the best way to achieve the educational aims of all students on all courses of study. But 82 institutions applied in the first year alone.

By being made corporations or companies, educational institutions will always be vulnerable to these moral dilemmas. It seems likely that increasingly the public sector will be dependent on tendering and sponsorship in this way. Both the PCFC and the UFC could use such methods.

Weakening the CNAA

Through its validation procedures, the CNAA has done an excellent job in raising the standards and status of public sector higher education (PSHE). ('Validation' is the process of evaluating a course in order to certify the standard of students who complete it successfully.) In effect the CNAA has considerable academic power. After twenty years it was in the government's and PSHE's interest to weaken its influence a bit.

In universities, course proposals are usually first considered by a working group and appropriate departmental staff. They are then more formally presented to a faculty board for criticism and amendment before formal approval by the university senate, the final arbiter on academic matters. After that there are a number of ongoing checks on the quality of courses, not least by the same working and departmental groups, the head of department, student opinion, reports of external examiners, and a whole network of contacts through postgraduates, employers, academic conferences and the like where its reputation is evaluated. However, until recently, most faculty boards and senates have not formally made regular checks on the quality of university courses after that.

In the polytechnics and other colleges in the public sector, all these quality controls exist, but there are more besides. In particular, while a college academic board may perform a function similar to a university senate within a public sector institution, it cannot award degrees. This has been done by the CNAA. The CNAA has also used peer review, but through a phalanx of subject committees whose members have been recruited from institutions across the whole country. The CNAA inspects public sector institutions every five years to report on their general suitability to provide degree-level courses. Public sector colleges are also open to inspection by local and national HMIs (Her Majesty's Inspectors). Specific course proposals needed to be validated by the CNAA before they could be provided and were regularly reviewed thereafter.

Understandably, this lack of independence, particularly compared with the universities, was felt by many public sector staff to be degrading. Furthermore, the pre-course validation always involved considerable delay in responding to employer and public demand. In addition some ill-informed local education authorities did not understand the academic freedoms necessary for higher education to flourish and some polytechnics complained bitterly of the strictures that local education committees imposed in academic matters. Consequently, some polytechnic directorates thought that control by central government was preferable.

By 1985, it was felt that the polytechnics had come of age and should be capable of awarding their own degrees. This process is directly analogous to the way many newer civic universities became independent in the 1950s, having previously taken degrees of the University of London. A committee, under the chairmanship of Sir Norman Lindop, a former director of Hatfield Polytechnic, recommended that there should be a range of forms of validation, including validating institutions, groups of individual courses, specific subject areas and complete self-validation. Each institution would apply for what it deemed appropriate to its particular stage of development. The CNAA itself had previously suggested partnership in validation.

The Lindop proposals would probably have been too diverse and messy. The government did not accept them but wanted some change. From 1988 onwards, polytechnics and other colleges could apply for independence to validate their own degrees for a period of five years.

What the Education Reform Act did

As expected the Education Reform Act 1988 swept away the University Grants Committee and the National Advisory Board and replaced them with the University Funding Council (UFC) and the Polytechnics and Colleges Funding Council (PCFC).

It turned polytechnics and colleges of higher education into free-standing statutory corporations. The polytechnics and colleges in question were any institution hitherto maintained by a local education authority, provided that: first, its amount of higher education work was equivalent to 350 full-time students; and second, that its higher education was over 55 per cent of its work. In practice eleven other colleges, mostly colleges of art, speech and drama, were made eligible to become corporations even though they didn't have 350 full-time equivalent higher education students.

As corporations in some ways they became like the British Broadcasting Corporation. The difference between the BBC and the polytechnics and colleges is that there is only one BBC, while there were 93 eligible polytechnics and colleges. The government therefore established the PCFC to apportion government funding 'for the provision of education, research and other activities . . . and for certain prescribed higher education courses'.

It is this prescription that makes the public sector under the PCFC different from the private university sector under the UFC. Otherwise it is hard to see much difference between the two Councils. Indeed twenty years earlier, polytechnics and colleges of education were seen as locally based teaching institutions. Now they are recognised as national (and indeed international) institutions doing research and offering consultancy like the universities.

Both the UFC and the PCFC have fifteen members of whom six to nine are appointed by the Secretary of State as having experience and competence in the field of higher education; while the remainder have experience in the fields of industry, commerce and finance.

The significance of this difference is, once again, to do with the extent of government control. In effect the government has taken powers to tell the polytechnics and colleges what they shall teach; while the universities, with their Royal Charters, are not vulnerable in this way. The government preserved the binary system in order to preserve its power. Otherwise the 'seamless robe' with one funding council supporting a wide variety of institutions each competing in a free market, might have seemed to be a policy more consistent with government policy.

There are, however, two other pertinent differences between the public and the private sectors. They are both concerned with the maintenance of the government's power. First, the Act empowers the government to change the instruments and articles of government of every maintained higher and further education institution providing full-time education. It also requires polytechnics and colleges to supply the Education Minister with any information he thinks he needs.

Summary

In this chapter I have tried to summarise 2,500 years of higher education. There is an underlying theme no matter how you balance the aims of higher education considered in Chapter 2: the search for, and the proclamation of, the truth as one sees it are the fundamental activities of higher education. They necessitate a freedom which has to be constantly guarded against the incursions of religion and the State.

While people through the centuries have had ideas fitting their time which have contributed to the shape of higher education today, there are also fundamental ideas about the nature of knowledge and how it is obtained which have burned like lanterns through the ages, sometimes brightly, sometimes dimly when blown by the wind. If ever they are blown out, our civilisation will suffer a loss of freedom and a loss of progress. To seek the truth is fundamental to freedom. To apply it is fundamental to progress.

Further reading

W. A. C. Stewart, *Higher Education in Postwar Britain* (Macmillan, 1989).

Chapter 4

UNDERSTANDING THE NEW
HIGHER EDUCATION SYSTEM

The government passed its Education Reform Act in 1988. It was supposed to create order while maintaining the diversity of institutions offering higher education in Britain. Yet to anyone looking at British higher education for the first time, that diversity will still inspire a sense of confusion. This chapter aims to clarify the picture.

The government defined higher education loosely in terms of courses above the standard of A-level GCE (General Certificate of Education). This definition includes part-time courses for Higher National Certificate (HNC) and full-time ones for Higher National Diploma (HND). It would also include many professional courses not supported by the public purse; but the Act wasn't concerned with them. The Act was mostly concerned with degree-level work; and there are around 350 colleges and other institutions that do some teaching at or above degree level. These institutions covered by the Act can be classified into two sectors: private and public. There are also institutions not covered by the Act doing some post-A-level work. They can also be divided into private and public colleges.

So higher education in Britain can be found in four kinds of institution. Most of it is in the first two, hence the emphasis in this book.

1. The private sector covered by the Act. That means institutions that were established by getting their own private charter from the Queen. Consequently they are all universities:

   (a) the universities funded by the UFC;

   (b) the independent universities of Cranfield and Buckingham; and

(c) the Open University (OU) funded by the DES.

2. Public sector higher education covered by the Act (PSHE) – that means institutions funded by public money. They include:

   (a) the polytechnics funded by the Polytechnics and Colleges Funding Council (PCFC);

   (b) colleges and institutes of higher education funded by the Polytechnics and Colleges Funding Council (PCFC) (all of these colleges have more than 55 per cent, or more than 350 full-time equivalent students doing work above A-level standard); and

   (c) the Scottish Central Institutions (CIs), including five colleges of education, funded by the Scottish Education Department (SED).

3. Private colleges not covered by the Act (such as Henley Management College and some satellite colleges of American universities).

4. Colleges not covered by the Act, with small amounts of higher education funded by public money, but not the PCFC.

The universities

The distinguishing feature of a university is that it is established by a charter from the sovereign. The terms of a charter can only be changed with the permission of the Queen's Privy Council. For this reason, like the government, universities are responsible to the Queen. Unlike universities in most other countries, they are not directly responsible to the government. In this sense they are private. Institutions responsible to local or national government are under public control. This constitutional position of universities is important to preserve their freedom from government interference and the freedom of ordinary people from government control of knowledge.

Universities are equally concerned to gain new knowledge and insights by research and scholarship as they are to teach. It is remarkable how many students arrive at university unaware of this dual function. Universities design, validate and administer their own courses, student assessments and awards. The vast majority of full-time students take degree courses leading to bachelor's, master's or doctoral degrees.

There are 50 universities in the UK – 47 partly funded by a newly established Universities Funding Council (UFC). Of the universities funded by the UFC, there are several different kinds resulting from their past history.

Oxbridge

Oxford and Cambridge are ancient universities founded in the Middle Ages each with many different colleges forming the university. Financially the colleges are relatively well endowed. The centres of both cities are dominated by the universities. College residences and a chapel are often round a courtyard, the entrance to which is past a porter's lodge and a scattered array of bicycles.

These universities have their own entrance examinations. Students apply to be resident at a college but there are also separate academic departments. Applicants with breadth, depth and the ability to argue their own point of view are most likely to be selected. These universities offer scholarships and exhibitions (minor scholarships) to the best applicants, the value of which lies more in their prestige than their monetary value.

Unlike other universities the central method of teaching is the university tutorial. Each student is assigned to a tutor for whom, typically, he writes a weekly essay, which is then critically discussed. Lectures have a supporting role and attendance is optional. This method develops individuality and independence of mind, articulate and balanced argument, the ability to research sources, and the capacity to work under pressure and to meet deadlines. It is expensive of staff time, but arguably worth it. It is an excellent training for the Civil Service, which is still remarkably dominated by Oxbridge graduates despite the growth of higher education elsewhere.

For many purposes St Andrews, on the east coast of Scotland, should be included with Oxbridge. It is not so large, nor does it have many different colleges; but it is the oldest university in Britain. Like Oxbridge, the university dominates the town. Indeed the town would scarcely exist if it were not for the university. It does not have the same method of selecting students, nor does it operate the same system of tutorial teaching; but it does offer some scholarships and it continues to attract good students, many of whom are English.

Other collegiate universities

Durham University, the third oldest, is also collegiate. So are the University of Wales with seven colleges, and London University, which is so enormous and scattered that its staff and students identify more with their college than their university. Many of the colleges have distinctive characters and their own international reputations for satisfying particular needs. For example Imperial College has a formidable reputation for research in science and technology. The London School of Economics (LSE) is equally respected among social scientists. Birkbeck has a unique place in the provision of part-time evening degrees. Bedford and Royal Holloway were the first women's colleges, though now merged on a site near Runnymede. As many as twelve medical schools have now merged to form six; some, like Guy's and St Thomas's, are better known to the general public than the University itself, so that ordinary people think of them only as hospitals, not as being part of a university. London University also includes numerous specialist institutions such as the Institute of Education, the Institute of Psychiatry, the School of Hygiene and Tropical Medicine and the Royal Veterinary College. All have made internationally recognised contributions in their fields.

The contributions of Oxbridge and London alone to the life of the nation are staggering, yet so diverse that they are not recognised.

Older civic universities

The older civic universities are those that sprang up at the end of the nineteenth century in the rapidly growing industrial cities. Some of them grew from the adult education and trade union movements of that time, when, it must be remembered, secondary education was not generally available. Edinburgh and Glasgow can also be included under this heading, though they are much older and have different origins.

Although older civic universities now see themselves as national, if not international, institutions, they retain some of their local interests (e.g. textiles at Leeds, music at Manchester, metallurgy at Sheffield). In particular they mostly have large extra-mural departments originally serving their local communities with cultural non-vocational evening and daytime classes. In the 1980s these departments have been allowed, indeed strongly encouraged, to provide vocational courses in what is now called 'continuing education'.

The older civic universities were sometimes called 'Red brick' universities. Their sites are not to be found in the central commercial business districts of their once thriving industrial cities, but just beyond, close enough to serve their adult communities. They may have been green field sites when the first red bricks were laid, but now, with the growth of cities and their own expansion, little grass can be seen. They are cramped for space. Much of their older accommodation is now inappropriate and expensive to maintain and heat.

After Oxbridge, older civic universities demand the highest entry standards, as measured by A-level scores. They are able to teach a very wide range of subjects because, by the post-Robbins expansion in the 1960s, they were already mature institutions with a broad academic base on which to build specialist departments in what were then new fields (e.g. subjects within the broad fields of biotechnology and the information sciences). Furthermore, when the cuts came, units that were cut to a non-viable size were able to find other departments with which they could sensibly merge, rather than close down. In younger and smaller universities, small units were more likely to have been closed with years of development work wasted, when there were no kindred units with which they could merge.

Newer civic universities

The newer civic universities were those (e.g. Exeter, Hull, Leicester, Nottingham, Reading and Southampton) whose students had taken London external degrees until the early 1950s. That was like a period of apprenticeship in which comparisons could be made between the standards of the various 'university colleges', as they were called, against the standards of London. During the 1950s they obtained charters and were able to award their own degrees. Newcastle had a similar apprenticeship with Durham and could best be placed in this group.

Some of them have developed specialist reputations. Some of these are associated with local industries, for example mechanical, production, electrical, electronic and aero-engineering at Southampton all contribute to the aircraft industry. Pharmacy at Nottingham has long been supported by Boots the chemists.

The newer civic universities could be divided into two groups on the basis of their subject balance. Ignoring expenditure in medical schools, Southampton, Reading, Nottingham and Newcastle spend slightly more on science than on arts; but Exeter, Hull and Leicester each spend about twice as much on arts as on science.

Some of the newer civic universities, for example Newcastle and Leicester, are like the older civics in that they occupy sites well within the built-up area of the city and they have built on all the available space. Some, such as Exeter and Hull, have green field sites, perhaps by taking a timely opportunity to move from humble beginnings in the city centre. This may mean that they have been multi-campus universities during a formative period.

New universities

In the post-war period, two new kinds of universities were established. There were 'new' universities, such as East Anglia and Sussex, which were usually on large greenacre sites outside medium-sized towns. Indeed, from 1957 to 1967 the availability of large sites was the main factor in deciding which towns and cities would be funded to build new universities.

Some of these universities were established with new ideals. Keele tried to tackle the problem of early specialisation by requiring all undergraduates to take a general course in their first year, followed by two subjects over a further three years. However the scheme did not attract large numbers of students. Sussex tried to break down the barriers between disciplines that sometimes exist in other universities, but in the research context academics in the same subject, talking the same language with the same background knowledge and overlapping interests, naturally tended to form groups in which others felt less comfortable. Warwick saw itself as a limited company and after an uncertain beginning, this policy has paid handsomely in the 1980s. Warwick is regarded as among the best for general engineering, computer science, biology, mathematics, economics, politics, sociology, French, history of art, and business management – not bad for a late starter!

Like Warwick other new universities have developed particular specialisms, for example sociology at Essex, management at Stirling, biochemistry at Dundee and social administration at York. These developments have often been the result of one individual who has attracted a lot of research money, attracted sponsorship and students when the rest of the university had difficulty, or so transformed a subject by his or her own insights that good staff and students are attracted to form a strong nucleus.

In short, 25 years after Robbins, the new universities have made their mark. Yet in the 1990s all may change: the young staff appointed 25 years ago are approaching the ages of early retirement. Sharp political changes may release new ideas, new methods and new areas for research – we cannot know.

Ex-CATs

The second kind of university established in the post-war period were the former Colleges of Advanced Technology (the ex-CATs) which were upgraded to university status following the report of the Robbins Committee in 1964. These, like Salford, Heriot-Watt, Strathclyde, City (London), Aston and Bradford, were often sited in the middle of industrial cities. Others, like Bath and the University of Surrey, which had been Battersea College of Technology, moved to green field sites.

Naturally the ex-CATs retained their former staffs – staffs who typically had already had ten years' experience in industry before joining the college during the late 1950s. Consequently many of them were not young researchers full of zest. Some may have resented being expected to do research when that was not part of the job they originally accepted. Some saw themselves as professionals with practical experience to pass on to students, rather than academics breaking new ground. So the research image of some ex-CATs was slow to develop.

There were also reasons why student numbers did not increase rapidly. First there was the swing against science in the late 1960s and early 1970s. The ex-CATs had few arts and humanities departments, and science applicants were more likely to be attracted to universities with established reputations. The city centre sites and local college origins of the ex-CATs meant that they had few student residences. As a result students have often had to choose between expensive rents or daily journeys from the suburbs, to be paid from ever-depreciating grants. These factors made them appear less popular among student applicants than other universities. For example, although they tended to recruit many more mature students with work experience and professional qualifications so that they had a richness of a different kind, on school-based entry qualifications they compared unfavourably with other universities.

Thus, through no fault of their own, in both research and teaching, some of the ex-CATs found reputations difficult to develop. So when cuts were necessary in 1981, there appeared to be academic reasons why some of the ex-CATs should suffer, in addition to the factors described in Chapter 3 to do with the proportion of staff near to retirement.

Public sector higher education covered by the Act (PSHE)

Although several mergers are imminent, at the time of writing there are 93 of these institutions. They all have over 55 per cent of their full-time students taking post-A-level courses and they mostly have many more. They can be divided into three groups.

First, there are 29 polytechnics in England and Wales. To these may be added Central Institutions of Scotland doing similar work such as Robert Gordon's College in Aberdeen, Glasgow College and Napier Polytechnic in Edinburgh.

Second, 39 others were under the control of local education

authorities until 1989. These former local education authority colleges are mostly institutes or colleges of higher education which used to be colleges of education training teachers or former colleges of art. The remainder consist of smaller, often rather specialist institutions.

The Polytechnics

When the polytechnics were first established in the early 1970s it was thought that they would be different from universities in that:

- they were financed by the local authority;
- their courses would be validated by the CNAA;
- their students would mostly be local;
- they would mostly teach science, technology and applied vocational subjects;
- they would build and maintain close relationships with local employers; and
- their effort would be devoted to teaching rather than research.

Since that time they have become more like universities in each of these characteristics.

- They are now financed nationally by the PCFC. They are mostly established as corporations limited by guarantee.
- Most of them now have much more independence in the validation of their degrees. Increasingly the CNAA is recognising the competence of polytechnics to maintain the quality of their courses without every modification being scrutinised by a CNAA committee, even though the CNAA may still be the (degree) awarding body. In effect a polytechnic as a whole is given a licence to operate for five years when its quality will again be reviewed.
- Although, like universities, polytechnics may recruit heavily from their own region, they are now largely seen as national institutions. Most polytechnics have grown from a local technical college or college of art which had no residential accommodation; and, as with the ex-CATs, most student applicants from a distance would not fancy rented accommo-

dation in an unknown inner city. However, in the late 1970s, as we shall see in a moment, many polytechnics absorbed a college of education. In these colleges there was a long tradition that students went away to college. The colleges had expanded in the 1960s and usually had residences built to a minimum standard. A wider catchment area for polytechnics aided recruitment to unusual courses and made them more viable. That in turn allowed polytechnics to develop their individuality.

- With the swing from science in the 1970s, and the heavy demand at the same time for low cost courses in the arts, humanities and business, the number of polytechnic students in these subjects far outstripped those in science and technology by 1980. This balance continues today.

- Although polytechnics still have more student placements in local industry and more sandwich courses than universities, courses with those features are less prominent in polytechnics now, while their prominence in universities is beginning to grow.

- Although they are not financed to do so, polytechnics have always encouraged their staffs to do research. Research in polytechnics is increasingly being published and recognised; and their staffs are increasingly prominent in academic and learned societies (not least because the cutbacks in university finance and escalating rail costs make it impossible for most university staffs to attend more than one conference a year from university funds).

In short, since they were established, the differences between polytechnics and universities have decreased. The Education Reform Act 1988 was a major opportunity for the government to create a unified system of higher education if it had wanted to. It was divided and chose not to. It reaffirmed the binary policies of the previous twenty years – possibly because they were policies that brought higher education under closer government control and preserved the elitism of universities.

Most polytechnics (for example East London) inherited old or inappropriate buildings in decaying parts of inner cities, but most local authorities viewed their polytechnics with pride and went to some expense to build or improve their physical facilities. For example, most of Bristol Polytechnic has moved to purpose-built accommodation on a green field site outside the city near to motorway and InterCity rail communications. North London Polytechnic, on the other hand, was formed from a merger of the former Northern and North-Western Polytechnics and continues to operate on five sites in buildings typical of the 1920s or earlier. Others had to make use of existing inner city sites so that new accommodation was built taller. Once built, the sites provided little opportunity for expansion, but in the mid-1970s, when there was pressure to close dozens of colleges of education, many of them (for example Birmingham, Manchester, Kingston, Oxford and Leeds) acquired pleasant facilities in suburban if not rural surroundings.

Managerially, mergers provide both opportunities and problems. They provide opportunities for new, original and exciting courses when merged staffs have complementary expertise. When they have similar expertise mergers may create a critical mass capable of creating a distinctive reputation. In practice human factors often intervene. It is not easy to develop working relationships with new colleagues when campuses are several miles apart. Nor is it usually possible for students to travel from one to another.

This section in the Education Reform Act covers a small number of colleges which have fewer than 350 students, but more than 55 per cent doing higher-level work. They include some former technical colleges, several colleges of art, colleges of speech and drama, and one college each specialising in music, agriculture and mining. The 93 PSHE institutions also include sixteen so-called 'voluntary colleges' which were mostly former colleges of education partly supported by religious denominations. Finally there are seven other colleges of music, agriculture and nursing.

The Education Reform Act does not apply to Scotland. In Scotland there are seventeen Central Institutions (CIs) funded by the Scottish Education Department. They display the same variety as those funded by the PCFC. For example, Robert Gordon's Institute of Technology is similar to a polytechnic, and Moray House, like an English college of higher education, is rapidly diversifying from its early specialisation in teacher training. There are others concentrating in certain fields, such as Queen Margaret's College in Edinburgh which serves the professions supplementary to medicine.

Private colleges not covered by the Act

These colleges are private, not in the sense that they have charters from the Queen – they don't, but in the sense that they are financed by private money. For example, management colleges charge good fees to the managers of industry, commerce and the professions. Ecclesiastical colleges, largely for training ministers of religion, are often supplemented by trusts and other endowments. And there are other colleges supported by particular interests, such as the trade unions, professions (such as the Inns of Court supported by the legal professions) and other interest groups.

There are also a number of colleges, such as Richmond College, which are satellite colleges of American universities. Students may come for a semester (half a year), continuing their degree courses, but also gaining experience of a culture other than their own.

Publicly funded colleges with small amounts of higher education

There are many regional and local colleges supported by local education authorities (LEAs) which have a large number of students, but only a small proportion studying above A-level standard. Typically some time in the past there may have been an ambitious head of department and local demand for a particular degree course or Higher National Diploma and the college may have sought validation from the CNAA or submitted its students for London external degrees. These LEA colleges also support large numbers of professional courses, for example in social work or business, which are above A level in standard, but which are not framed in the academic mould.

In addition there are a large number of professional training establishments which are supported by other government departments, not the DES or the SED. For example the schools of nursing, physiotherapy, occupational therapy and other professions supplementary to medicine receive grants from the Department of Health.

Consequences of the Act

No doubt the consequences of the Act are far reaching. I want to pick on two: institutional linkage and contractual relationships.

Institutional links

Over the last two centuries the system has grown. Broadly speaking, in any of groups 1, 2 and 4 (see pp. 50–1) older institutions have had more time to build larger departments and more of them, while colleges specialising in, for example, art or music, are likely to have remained small. The finance of small colleges of this kind is likely to be difficult when the number of student applications fluctuates.

Consequently, throughout the UK beginning in Northern Ireland, mergers, federations and special relationships between institutions have been, or are being, developed, often with government encouragement. For example most colleges of education are seeking links with universities or polytechnics. Since the publication of *Project 2000*, schools of nursing under a certain size are likely to lose government funding. So they too, are under pressure to merge with each other or some other institution. There are many other bilateral arrangements. For example, virtually all courses run by Duncan of Jordanstone College of Art are now validated by Dundee University. In short, the map of higher education is being redrawn.

Contractual relationships

In future the UFC, the PCFC and the government will increasingly give money for specific purposes. Although on the surface universities have retained their former independence, the binary system has been preserved, and the polytechnics now have increased independence because they have become public corporations, in practice they will increasingly only be financed to do what their paymasters want. Grants will be reduced; contractual agreements will increase.

The consequences are unpredictable. When the government first gave grants to universities, the system assumed an element of trust. Universities were allowed to spend the money as they thought fit. There was a spirit of goodwill. Governments and many others in the community sought the advice of academics who gave their time unstintingly without payment. A price was not put on everything, not least because it cannot be – particularly in education. It was assumed that education was as much about moral development – honesty, commitment, persuasion, concern for others and dedication – as about knowledge, its application, judgement, open-mindedness and the capacity to seek the truth.

The contractual relationship assumes not only that a monetary value can be put on these things, but that we can know who benefits from them and ought to pay. Who benefits from there being people with historical knowledge? Answer: we all do. So the government will pay to retain the study and teaching of history. But who decided that our society benefits from this knowledge – someone in the Civil Service controlling our knowledge?

The contractual relationship gives power over our minds to those who have money. For example, history is in favour, but sociology is not. History generates criticism of past governments. Sociology generates criticism of existing ones. Research funds for sociology have been axed.

The implications of these changes need to be understood by members of the public, not least the readers of this book. Democracy can only survive when knowledge is freely available.

Further reading

Department of Education and Science, *Higher Education – meeting the challenge*, Cmd 114 (HMSO, 1987).

Chapter 5

IS IT WORTH ENTERING HIGHER EDUCATION?

Yes it is. That's a generalisation. Of course it depends on individual factors. This chapter is concerned with the individual's decision to apply. Obviously it cannot answer personal questions. Nonetheless, in coming to a decision there are questions that intending students, their parents or spouses will want answered: 'What are the costs and benefits?', 'Will the student gain in the long run?' and 'What are the chances of getting in, anyway?'

This chapter aims to give facts that will help to answer these questions. The next chapter looks at the decisions taken by admissions tutors and others in higher education, affecting whether applications are accepted.

What are the costs and benefits?

In 1987 the Department of Education and Science carried out surveys of students' income and expenditure over the 38 weeks from October to June. So one way to answer this question is to present a summary account (Table 5.1). Inflation may make the sums out of date, but the proportions under each heading should be informative to intending applicants and their parents (figures are rounded to the nearest pound). The surveys were confined to single undergraduates under the age of 26.

The survey was constructed to balance income and expenditure. As you see, it does not. The researchers attribute this to inaccuracies of 3 per cent in students' responses.

Certain points stand out clearly. Although students are adults, they are heavily dependent on parental support. Indeed, compared with a survey four years earlier by the National Union of Students, student grants and awards not only failed to keep pace with inflation, they actually fell. Cor-

Table 5.1   Student income and expenditure 1986–87

Income	£
Grants and awards	1,120
Parental support	1,113
Own income	119
Board provided by parents	114
Loans	99
Drawings on savings	96
Social Security benefits	91
Gifts from relatives	49
Total income	**2,801**

Expenditure	£
Rent	779
Food and common household expenses	462
Entertainment, tobacco and alcohol	399
Leisure travel and motoring	227
Books, equipment and course travel	172
Payment for parental accommodation	114
Travel to college	115
Clothing	132
Gifts	118
Fuel	56
Post and telephone	56
Miscellaneous	252
Total	**2,882**

Source: Top-up Loans for Students (HMSO, 1988).

respondingly the contribution of parents has had to rise from
£492 to £1,113. Taking the two surveys together, around 40
per cent of students whose parents were assessed as able to
make a contribution, did not receive it in full. Students need
to do some academic work during the summer and to see a bit
of the world, but they also need other income. During the 1986
summer vacation students' average income was £476; 59 per
cent got an average of £531 from an average of eight weeks'

work; while 58 per cent claimed benefits also for an average of eight weeks with an average income of £193 (10 per cent did neither; 27 per cent did both).

Up to 1990 students' financial position deteriorated, but British graduates were also expensive for the taxpayer. If higher education was to expand, and since early 1989 it was widely agreed that it should, a new method of financing undergraduates had to be found. The government devised a top-up loans scheme. It includes many features from the former grants scheme. So I shall first describe the grants scheme up to 1990 and then the top-up loans scheme.

The system of student grants up to 1990

Tuition fees were paid by local education authorities (LEAs) for all full-time students on first degree courses, certain other university certificates and diplomas, the Diploma in Higher Education (DipHE), Higher National Diplomas (HNDs) and initial teacher training. These were called 'mandatory awards' because the LEA was compelled to pay them.

Mandatory awards were not available for part-time students because it was assumed that in the rest of their time they were earning enough to pay for themselves. They were not available to students who had previously received an award when taking another course, nor to students who had lived abroad during the previous three years.

In addition to tuition fees, the award was a contribution to maintenance costs. For students living in their parents' home in 1989 the maintenance award was £1,630. For those living elsewhere the maintenance element was £2,050 (£2,425 in London). The maintenance element was assumed to cover the Christmas and Easter vacations as well as 30 weeks of term time. Hence it did not cover the summer vacation.

Students over the age of 24 were regarded as independent of their parents. So were those who had been married or earning for three years.

The size of the maintenance element depended upon what was called the parents' 'residual income'. This was calculated by taking the parents' total income and making deductions to allow for adult dependants, interest payments (including their mortgage), and superannuation, life insurance and pension scheme contributions. The amount parents could contribute to the student's maintenance was then calculated and further reductions were made for other dependent children, including others who were receiving higher education. There was a sliding scale of parental contributions as shown in Table 5.2. The maximum annual contribution for most parents was limited to £4,900.

Table 5.2 Parental contributions in relation to their residual income 1986–87

Parents' residual income[1]	0 to 8,700	8,700 to 11,100	11,100 to 14,000	14,000 to 16,200	16,200 to 18,300	18,300+
Assessed parent contribution[2]	0	20 to 350	350 to 950[3]	950 to 1,400	1,400 to 1,900[4]	1,900+

Notes:
1. Parental contributions were based on residual incomes for the previous year.
2. Contributions may have been less where there were other dependent children.
3. Contribution changed from £1 in £7 of residual income to £1 in £5.
4. Contribution changed from £1 in £5 of residual income to £1 in £4.

The top-up loans scheme

The top-up loans will gradually pay for more and more of students' costs. The parental contribution and the LEA award will be kept at the same figures from now onwards. This means that with inflation their real value will progressively decrease.

To compensate for that decrease, the value of the loans will progressively increase both in the amount of cash and as a proportion of the students' total income. The portion of a student's income from a government loan will be allowed to increase until it is equal to the parental contribution and mandatory award added together. In other words a loan will never be more than half a student's income. (You may ask 'What will the government do when that point is reached?' The government's reply is that it will decide nearer the time. It said that will be in the year 2007 assuming that the average annual rate of inflation over the seventeen-year period from 1990 is maintained at 3 per cent. How the government made that assumption I shall leave to your imagination!)

Loans are offered at a rate of interest equivalent to inflation. In other words, in real terms the rate of interest will be zero.

Students are normally required to start repaying the loan in the April following the end of their period of study; but the repayment may be deferred when the individual's personal income is low (a spouse's income will not be taken into account). The government is anxious that an inability to repay should not discourage applications to enter higher education. In particular the decision to interrupt work in order to raise children should not be constrained by any obligation for repayment; nor should low income careers (e.g. a career in the Church). However a limit will be imposed in cases where repayments are repeatedly deferred because of low income. The loan will be written off in the event of death, the recipient reaching the age of 50, or 25 years after the loan commenced, whichever is the sooner. (Students starting courses over the age of 40 will be expected to repay by the age of 60.) Because the government considers the aims of higher education purely in career terms, it is not offering loans to students over the age of 50.

Students in higher education are no longer eligible for income support, unemployment benefit or housing benefit. However, disabled students, those who are single parents and partners of students will remain eligible for benefits. Support for students' dependants will also continue.

The loans scheme has been opposed on a number of grounds. Loans, it is said, will be a particular disincentive to disadvantaged groups. But in other matters lower social classes depend on credit as much, or more than professional classes. Why should higher education be different? Mature students with families incur debts under the present system; they should find the interest rates of the loans scheme more attractive than present commercial alternatives. The scheme tries to allow for the needs of women and the low paid.

The top-up loans scheme also provides three access funds each of £5 million to provide discretionary support for individual cases of financial need:

- for those within the scope of the loans provision with or without mandatory grants;
- for postgraduates; and
- for students in further education.

Will the student gain in the long run?

Yes. The answer to this question is usually given by economists. Their discipline requires them to answer the question in terms of gains that are tangible and measurable. But it should always be remembered that not all the gains of higher education are of that kind. I cannot prove it, but I think most students enjoy the rest of their lives better because they matured in certain ways when at college.

Graduates have a better chance of getting a job and they get better jobs. The unemployment rate for graduates has always been less than for their age group in the population as a whole. It fell throughout the 1980s. At the end of 1987 it was 6 per cent for universities and 9 per cent for polytechnics. The patterns of employment for former university and polytechnic full-time students on degree courses are very similar, except that university students without a permanent job seem to be better at getting a temporary one.

Not surprisingly students who take vocational subjects are more likely to be employed six months after completing their courses. In subjects like education, engineering, medicine and business studies the number with jobs is around 80 per cent whether they went to universities or polytechnics. In non-vocational subjects such as the arts, humanities, the social sciences, the physical sciences and biology around 45 per cent had permanent employment.

Parents should recognise that a student's education is not always finished when he or she graduates. They may need to budget for this. About a quarter of all graduates take some kind of further education or training. In the physical and biological sciences over a quarter stay in research or some other kind of academic study; 5 per cent will enter teacher training and about another 15 per cent training for some other specific job, making 45 per cent in all. In arts, humanities and the social sciences over 30 per cent take some form of job-specific training apart from teaching.

It is clear that graduates earn more money than non-graduates with A levels who did not enter higher education. Those gains last the rest of their lives. On the other hand the cost of not earning while studying must be offset against those gains. Of course it is possible that those who choose to enter higher education have some innate or social abilities that would have brought them better salaries anyway. Some allowance can be made for this. The extent to which it pays to enter higher education depends on how much importance the economists attach to this; but if you consider the sums spent by students and others on their higher education as an investment and then consider the rate of return upon that investment, government economists calculate that graduates are 20–25 per cent better off, throughout their lives, than non-graduates with A levels. For arts students it is about 9 per cent, for scientists around 20 per cent and for engineers and social scientists between 25 per cent and 30 per cent. Of course there are considerable variations within these groups. For example, accountants earn very much better salaries than sociologists, although they are both classified as social scientists.

Another interesting and important factor is that the financial benefits of studying the arts and social sciences are longer delayed than for graduates in science and engineering, but are greater in the long run. In fact their salaries overtake the earnings of scientists and engineers by about the age of 28 for those students who enter higher education at the age of 18.

In doing these calculations the government has been concerned with another issue. It is less concerned with the question of whether it pays to enter higher education than with how much of the benefit goes to the students and how much to the rest of society. On their calculations most of the benefit goes to the students. That is used as an argument for saying that students should pay more of the costs of their higher education.

The weakness of this argument is, once again, that their calculations only include benefits that can be measured in terms of money such as graduates' increased earnings and the increased profitability of industry when it employs graduates. But as we saw in Chapter 2, the really important gains from higher education are not so tangible. They are to do with people's feelings, the maintenance of democracy and the benefits of having educated and cultured people outside the workplace, not least in the home and in the family. When considering educational issues, the reader should be constantly vigilant against assuming that money is the only thing that matters in our lives.

What are the chances of getting in anyway?

Most of all it depends upon qualifications. The A-level score out of 15 is obtained by taking an applicant's three best A-level results, scoring 5 for an A grade, 4 for a B, and so on. Look at Table 5.3 to see what percentage got in to British universities with each A-level score in 1988.

Table 5.3 Percentage of applicants accepted within A-level bands

A-level score	3–5	6–8	9–10	11–12	13–15
Accepted (%)	7	37	73	87	90

The introduction of AS levels (Advanced Supplementary) in 1989 has changed the scoring system. AS levels are at the same standard as A levels, but have half the content and require half the study time. They will score half as much. So they are now scored as 5 for an A, 4 for a B, and so on, and A-level scores are out of 30, with 10 for an A, 8 for a B, 6 for a C and so on.

The chances of getting in also depend upon the amount of competition. That varies for different subjects. Table 5.4 gives the proportion of applicants accepted for the largest subject groups.

You might think that where there are a lot of candidates for the number of places that can be offered, the average A-level score of accepted candidates would be higher. The table shows that that is not true so far as broad subject areas are concerned. There is not a lot of competition between subject areas.

Table 5.4   Percentage accepted and average A-level score of new entrants in major academic subjects in 1988–89

Subject group	Accepted (%)	Average A-level score accepted
Physical sciences	77	10.4
Maths and computing	66	11.5
Engineering	62	10.7
Languages	60	11.3
Biology	59	10.0
Humanities	59	11.1
Agriculture	51	10.0
Medicine and dentistry	44	12.8
Social sciences	40	11.6
Architecture, building, planning	34	10.5
Creative arts	34	10.2
Topics related to medicine	34	10.9
Education	31	8.0
Business	27	11.6
Total for all subjects	49	11.1

Source: UCCA, 27th Report.

That does not mean that there is little competition between institutions. There is, but it is not intense. There is a lot of overlap between institutions so far as the grades they accept are concerned. Taking the groups of universities discussed in Chapter 4, we can say, as a generalisation, that Oxbridge receives candidates with the highest scores (average 12–14). The average entry qualifications at the collegiate universities vary markedly with the college and the subject of study. The older civic (9–12), new civic, new and ex-CAT universities accept students with average scores descending in that order, but there is not much difference between them.

In the polytechnics less than 28 per cent of those who applied in 1988 were accepted, but that does not mean that the entry qualifications required were higher. A typical A-level score for successful candidates was between 5 and 9 varying with the subject and the polytechnic. So on the whole, universities are still able to demand higher A levels. But most polytechnics have developed some prestigious departments commanding higher entry standards. Therefore intending applicants should find out about specific departments before deciding where to apply. A similar pattern between institutions exists in Scotland where candidates gain admission a year earlier at 17, on the basis of up to half a dozen Higher School Certificate subjects.

There is nothing to stop a candidate applying to enter both universities and polytechnics. In 1988, 146,000 people applied to polytechnics and 184,000 to the universities; but 85,000 were the same people. Of these common applicants, 20,000 eventually went to polytechnics and 32,000 to universities. Another 20,000, who did not apply to the universities, went to polytechnics.

Obviously the chances of getting in are also affected by decisions taken by people in higher education. The next chapter aims to give an understanding of the factors influencing their decisions.

Further reading

Department of Education and Science, *Top-up Loans for Students* (HMSO, 1988).

Chapter 6

ACCESS TO HIGHER EDUCATION

Why are applications made through clearing houses?

It's efficient. You might think that if students want to enter higher education, they should simply write to the institutions of their choice, obtain prospectuses and return completed application forms to the institutions. If an application looks promising, the applicant may be invited for an interview, after which an offer might be made.

That is how you apply for most jobs. Indeed there are still a few colleges where that is the procedure. But consider it from the institution's point of view. You will soon see that the workload is vastly greater than any employer would normally have to bear. The number of students arriving every year is three or four times the number of academic staff. On average there are five times as many applicants as there are students who eventually start the following autumn. So the average higher education institution has fifteen to twenty times as many applicants each year as there are academic staff who can select them. Compared with any normal company that is a heavy workload.

Most colleges don't mind spending a lot of time selecting the right students because getting the wrong ones takes far more time in the long run. On the other hand it really is a waste of time to interview applicants who will probably get an offer from somewhere else where they would much prefer to go. For that reason a central clearing house system was introduced. Applicants may get prospectuses from the institutions of their choice, but completed applications are returned to a central clearing house. Another reason for clearing houses was to help rejected applicants find last-minute vacancies.

There are separate clearing houses for the universities (the Universities Central Council on Admissions – UCCA), for the polytechnics (the Polytechnics Central Admissions system – PCAS), for art and design (the Art and Design Admissions Registry), for teacher training courses in England and Wales (the Central Register), for teacher education in Scotland (the Teacher Education Admission Clearing House – TEACH) and for courses in physiotherapy (the Central Admissions Department for Physiotherapy Students at the Chartered Society of Physiotherapy).

The clearing houses handle all applications for full-time and sandwich first degree, Diploma in Higher Education and Higher National Diploma courses. Each clearing house has its own application forms. Applications for other courses should be made directly to the university, polytechnic or other institution concerned. Students normally apply to up to five universities but they can apply to as many polytechnics as they wish.

Polytechnics have a code of practice on student admissions. This includes providing adequate information about courses normally not later than June of the academic year prior to admission. Colleges normally give applicants an opportunity to visit the college, either as part of the selection process or after an offer has been made. An acceptance should depend upon the probability of completing the course successfully. So don't think that handicapped students need not apply. Each institution should have a member of staff able to advise on problems faced by handicapped students, including advising on how problems can be overcome. General advice can also be obtained from publications such as *Where?* and *Which Degree?*

On what criteria are applicants selected?

There is no fixed answer to this question. Each institution, indeed each faculty or department, will have its own criteria and procedures. Nevertheless, some generalisations can be made.

How important are applicants' academic qualifications?

Very important, except at the Open University (OU). Although Oxbridge has its own entrance examinations, Advanced Level General Certificates of Education (A levels) remain the most common entry qualification to higher education. They are mostly obtained at school or colleges of further education catering for 16- to 19-year-olds. Excluding overseas and OU students, if we take all those who entered universities in 1988 aiming for a first degree or diploma, 81 per cent gained entrance on the basis of their A levels. Another 10 per cent had Scottish Higher School Certificates; 4 per cent had certificates from the Business and Technician Education Council (BTEC) or its Scottish equivalent (SCOTVEC); 1 per cent had a degree already; about 3 per cent entered with other UK qualifications; while among the remainder, some had other professional or overseas qualifications, and others entered under special conditions. In the case of the polytechnics, just less than 70 per cent of new degree and diploma students entered with A levels. They took very few graduates, Scottish or overseas students for 'first' degrees. Almost all the remaining 30 per cent either had professional qualifications including certificates from BTEC, or special entry conditions. The Open University accepts students without any academic qualifications. That's why it is 'open'.

That raises a different question: Are A levels any good for selecting students? For example, do A-level scores predict the class of degree students eventually get? Figure 6.1 shows the relationship of degree class to students' A-level entry scores. It may be seen that there is a strong relationship between scores of 12 and over, and obtaining a first-class honours degree. There is also a positive relationship between A-level scores and the chances of getting an upper second-class degree or better. Although people with low A-level scores are more likely to drop out before obtaining their degree, the chances of people with poor A levels getting a degree of some kind are not markedly worse than those with good A levels. The truth is, if you are good enough to be admitted to a university, you are good enough to get a degree if you work reasonably hard. The factors that prevent students from working are more often social and emotional than academic.

Will going to a private school help an applicant's chances?

Not really. Some parents spend a lot of money sending their children to private schools in the belief that they are more

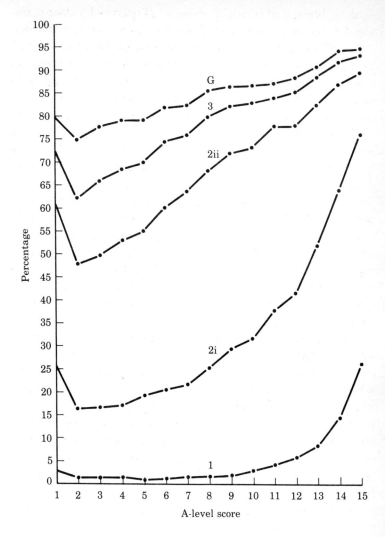

Notes
1. Percentage who obtained a first-class degree
2i Percentage who obtained a 2i-class degree or better
2ii Percentage who obtained a 2ii-class degree or better
3 Percentage who obtained a third-class degree or better
G Percentage who obtained a degree (graduated)

Figure 6.1 The relationship of A levels to class of degree obtained

likely to gain university entrance and do well at university once they get in. Unfortunately there is very little evidence to suggest that applicants from private schools do any better. The A-level profiles of successful applicants from private and comprehensive schools are identical. So is their degree performance, with the exception of graduates in arts subjects. Indeed in the 1970s, before grammar and other secondary schools merged to become comprehensive schools, it was clear from A-level and degree results that grammar school pupils out-performed those from private schools both at school and at university.

How important is the headteacher's reference?

It varies. Admission tutors look at headteachers' reports about pupils and they take some notice of them. Yet headteachers are different. They have different personalities and attitudes. They create schools with different climates in which the same pupil would respond differently. It is hard to believe that one headteacher's report will reflect the same standards as another. So how far an admissions tutor relies on the headteacher's opinion will vary with the tutor.

How much depends on the interview?

A lot, where they operate. Institutions wouldn't bother if they didn't think interviews were important. Some universities and colleges don't interview. They find that interviewers' judgements don't add enough to justify the time and expense. Some of these make standard offers and invite applicants to an open day. Others interview with great thoroughness, not least for courses concerned with interpersonal skills such as teaching, nursing, social work and management.

Many admissions tutors, particularly at Oxbridge, look for students who have original ideas and can defend them against criticism. But it would be a mistake to suppose that interviewers have fixed criteria. Quite often admissions tutors want to admit a mix of students. Variety can result in more mutual criticism and more learning from each other. The best advice to applicants is 'Have confidence to be yourself. Your opinion is worth hearing.'

Does learning from experience count for nothing?

It will count more and more. As we shall see later, there are good reasons to encourage mature adults without formal qualifications to seek higher education. When it is obvious that they have the ability, it is foolish and insulting to ask them to spend years obtaining school-based entry qualifications. What is needed is some way to assess prior experiential learning (APEL). There are four steps in this process. First, the college and applicant should reflect and identify what learning from experience has been significant. Second, the college needs to identify which claimed experiences are assessable. Then all the available evidence needs to be considered together to judge its value. Finally, an assessment and accreditation may be offered.

There are other kinds of useful experience that are not formally assessed. So the question is sometimes asked, 'Would I do better if I delay a year before going into higher education?' By delaying, students get graduate earnings one year later and, in that sense, they will miss one year's earnings. On the other hand, research has shown that those who delay a year have lower failure rates in their first and third years at university (many universities do not have examinations in the second year). Furthermore, most people who obtain useful experience before going to university say how valuable it has been. Others report that their career choices are more clear and, in some cases, employers are willing to contribute to their fees.

What are students like? Is it easy to fit in?

All kinds of people are students; so anyone who gets a place should be able to fit in somewhere. Being a student today is a serious and responsible undertaking involving a lot of hard work. At one time when students were thought to be the idle sons and daughters of gentlemen who would eventually become the elite of the nation, students were respected. Their pranks were tolerated. The poverty of those from lowly status was understood.

That belief was probably never accurate and has rightly disappeared. But with the manifold expansion of higher education and the development of student protest movements that are well organised, a more negative and equally inaccurate image is commonplace. It is the image my neighbour had in Chapter 1.

These perceptions are subjective. What are the facts? Students have probably been more thoroughly researched than any other group of the same size in our society. Students have a range of personal characteristics that relate to their behaviour and performance: for example their age, sex, social class, intelligence, their personality and motivation; the jobs they go to, and whether anyone else in their family has experienced higher education. They also vary in their academic characteristics: such as their entry qualifications; their subject of study; whether they are full-time or part-time; whether they are postgraduates or undergraduates, seeking certificates, diplomas or no qualifications at all; their life-style and study habits; and the extent of their eventual success or failure.

Although students are well researched, because most institutions in the public sector have been under the control of local and regional governments, or are voluntary aided by religious or other groups, national statistics are much more difficult to obtain than for the universities. In addition, personal data are not collected for continuing education students. Therefore, what follows may seem unduly biased towards university full-time students.

How many students are there in higher education?

At the end of December 1988, there were 961,000 students in British universities (excluding the OU). Of these, 579,000 were enrolled in continuing education, 98,000 were postgraduates and 275,000 were full-time undergraduates, 268,000 aiming for their first degree, and 7,000 aiming for other awards. Ten thousand undergraduates and 40,000 postgraduates were part-time.

In the public sector, there were 536,000 students on award-bearing courses in 1987–88, 35,000 were postgraduates, 220,000 were undergraduates aiming for their first degree and 281,000 were taking courses below degree level.

Table 6.1 Numbers of students on award-bearing courses

	Academic Year			
	1987/8² Public sector higher education	1989 Open University	1988/9 Other universities	1987/8² Total
	(Figures in thousands)			
Full-time students	303		334	609¹
Part-time students	233	85	50	359
Home initial entrants				
Under 21 (full-time)	63		70	126
Over 21 (full-time)	34		10	44
Overseas students³	15		49	59
Home students (full-time)	288		285	550
Home students (part-time)	233	85	50	359
Men home students				
(full-time)	157		193	337
(part-time)	150	45	29	219
Women home students				
(full-time)	147		141	272
(part-time)	83	40	21	140
Level of course				
Postgraduate (full-time)	15		58	70
Postgraduate (part-time)	20	4	40	56
First degree (full-time)	195		268	441
First degree (part-time)	25	71	7	102
Sub-degree (full-time)	93		7	98
(part-time)	188	11¹	3	202

Notes:
1. The figures are rounded to the nearest thousand. They do not include continuing education students in universities. In the Open University in 1989 there were also 12,000 Associate short course students.
   Sources: Universities Statistical Record and Open University.
2. *Source: Aim Higher – widening access to higher education* (Royal Society of Arts, 1989).
3. Students whose usual place of residence is outside the UK. All part-time students are treated as home students.

When you ask how big a particular university is, or how many students there are at a certain polytechnic, the answer you generally get is the number of full-time students. So it is worth noticing that over half the students in universities are part-time in continuing education. Of course, the vast majority are not taking advanced courses leading to recognised qualifications and if the amount of time they spend was converted into the equivalent of full-time students (FTE) their total would be less than the full-timers'. The number of part-timers in the public sector is also much greater than many people imagine.

Table 6.2 Home students by subject for academic year 1987/88 (in thousands)

	Polytechnics and colleges		Universities	
	F/time	P/time	F/time	P/time
Education	37	24	10	9
Medicine	11	9	29	4
Engineering and technology	44	63	34	3
Agriculture	2		5	
Science	42	17	64	6
Business and social studies	75	107	62	8
Professional and vocational	21	6	5	4
Languages	8	2	31	3
Other arts	15	4	3	21
Music, drama, art and design	34	2	5	

Source: Aim Higher – widening access to higher education (Royal Society of Arts, 1989).

Have most students come straight from school?

No, though most full-time students have. Table 6.3 shows the age and sex distribution of students on award-bearing courses in British higher education. It does not include half a million continuing education students, almost all of whom are over 25, and of whom many are over 60, who were not aiming for degrees, diplomas and certificates.

Notice that one in six of the full-time students is aged 25 or over, while 40 per cent are aged 21 or more. These figures may surprise many people who think of higher education as a continuation from school. Notice, too, that there are nearly a quarter of a million part-time students who are over the age of 24. In fact, 35 per cent of all students seeking qualifications in higher education are over the age of 24 and 61 per cent are 21 or more. Continuing education is growing and these figures will increase.

The majority (55 per cent) of university full-time under-graduates enter under the age of 19, including 6 per cent (mostly in Scotland where Higher School Certificates are taken one year after O grades) under 18. Another 25 per cent enter when they are 19. This could mean that the other 20 per cent have some experience other than school. Depending on what proportion of the 25 per cent of 19-year-olds have spent time doing something else, the figure could be much higher. The proportion is larger than many people would suppose and in polytechnics it is higher. Universities welcome students with life experience. Nonetheless, a greater proportion of older students do not have formal qualifications and find acceptance more difficult for that reason. In fact, over half the applicants to universities over the age of 19 are not accepted, while less than half of those aged 19 or younger fail to gain admittance.

Table 6.3 Age and sex distribution (per cent) of full- and part-time students on award-bearing courses in 1987/88

Age	Men (%)		Women (%)		Total (%)	
	Full-time	*Part-time*	*Full-time*	*Part-time*	*Full-time*	*Part-time*
Under 19	15	4	47	2	16	3
19 or 20	37	13	40	7	38	11
21 to 24	31	21	28	17	30	19
Over 24	17	63	16	74	16	67
Raw totals (in thousands)	346.1	224.1	280.8	142.5	626.9	366.6

Source: Social Trends, Volume 20.

The proportion of older applicants for degree and diploma courses has been steadily increasing since 1984. The proportion of mature applicants over the age of 25 has always been greater in arts and humanities than in the sciences (e.g. social administration 28 per cent, sociology 27 per cent, theology 26 per cent, philosophy 19 per cent, psychology 17 per cent, and combinations within the social sciences 16 per cent). Mature students can attain the same levels in quantitative subjects as younger students, but they often take longer to get there. For this reason, and because of financial and family commitments, they would do better if they were offered five-year half-time courses, rather than three-year full-time ones.

Is everyone in higher education very intelligent?

No one gives students intelligence tests as a regular thing; so any generalisations about students' intelligence have to be made by piecing evidence together from research where intelligence tests have been used. The short answer is ' "above average", Yes. "Very intelligent", No.'

You might think that students have to be quite intelligent to gain access to higher education; and they do; but there are quite a lot of people who don't enter higher education who are equally intelligent. So it would be quite wrong to think that all the best of British youth is creamed off for higher education. Some of the best are, some are not. Roughly speaking, university students are selected from the top 25 per cent of their age group in terms of intelligence. But until recently, when the size of the age group began to fall, only 8 per cent entered full-time university undergraduate courses. That means that roughly two people do not enter university for every one of equal intelligence who does. Another 7 per cent enter the public sector of higher education from roughly the top 30 per cent.

If intelligence is relevant one might conclude that the nation is not developing about half of its potential resources for higher education.

Until 1989, government arguments about the need to cut back on student numbers, based upon the falling number of 18-year-olds, assumed that there is a limited pool of ability which we successfully drain dry. That is not true. There is not a limited pool and we don't recruit all of the best. A certain amount of intelligence is necessary to be successful in higher education, but once above that level, there is not a close relationship between intelligence test scores and degree performance. A great deal of motivation, study skills and personal adjustment to college life are also needed. Standardised tests of academic aptitude have been successful in selecting students for college education in the USA because over half of the age group in that country goes to college, and the range of abilities to be discriminated is wide. The British system is far more selective and other qualities are required.

Is everyone in higher education upper- or middle-class?

No, but higher education should welcome many more working-class students. Table 6.4 shows the distribution of social class groups in British universities in 1988, according to the occupation of the students' fathers. It shows a disproportionate number in social classes I and II. We can ask 'Why is that?' One simple answer is to say that students inherit some of the abilities of their fathers and that jobs classified in groups I and II are more likely to be held by people with good intellectual abilities than jobs classified in groups IV and V. Another explanation is that children are more likely to sense an expectation that they should go to college from parents in social groups I and II than those who have parents in lower social groups. Such expectations are particularly strong if the parents have experienced higher education themselves.

These two explanations are different, though compatible. One makes assumptions about heredity, the other about social expectations in the students' environments. Although the two explanations may both be correct, they have different implications for educational policies. If we want to maximise the intellectual resources available to the nation, while we cannot influence the heredity of our schoolchildren very much, we can influence their expectations and aspirations.

There are some subjects (e.g. medicine) where it is quite common for students to follow in their fathers' footsteps. In arts and humanities, there is a tendency, not for students to study the same subject as their fathers, but for them to enter a similar faculty. Social class also influences choice of subjects. Children from working-class backgrounds are more likely to take engineering, part-time or non-degree courses, than anthropology, philosophy or Greek.

Table 6.4 Social class distribution of university students' fathers in 1988 compared with the distribution in the population as a whole

Social class	In UK population (%)	In UGC universities (%)	In OU (%)
I Professional	4.6	21.0	11.9
II Managerial	25.1	48.1	25.0
IIIA Skilled non-manual	24.5	11.0	18.0
IIIB Skilled manual	23.7	12.5	31.9
IV Partly skilled	16.6	6.3	7.7
V Unskilled	5.5	1.1	5.5

Note: The figures for the Open University (OU) are for 1981.

Environmental influence has a lot to do with perceptions, including self-perceptions. For example, when the Bath Regional College of Technology changed to a College of Advanced Technology and then to a university, the proportion of students from working-class origins decreased, even though the buildings, the staff and the level of work changed very little. It seems as if working-class students saw the university as beyond them, while the college of technology was not.

There are two other explanations for the imbalance in social origins of students. One is that universities and colleges are biased when accepting applicants. But the simple fact is that applicants from the higher social classes have better A-level grades. When allowance is made for this, there is remarkably little difference in the percentage of applicants accepted from each of these social class groups.

The other explanation is that the statistics might be wrong in some way. For example, people in lower social class groups are less likely to reveal their occupation. Consequently, these groups might be under-represented in the statistics. Furthermore, a disproportionate number of mature students have fathers in the lower social groups, but by the time they apply, they themselves have held occupations that would place them higher than their parents. This is illustrated in the figures for the OU. The figures based upon the occupation of OU students themselves are similar to the middle column in Table 6.5. This suggests that OU students are upwardly mobile.

Another source of error is that deciding a student's social class from the occupation of his or her father, rather than the mother, is a little arbitrary. In only one-third of cases are they classified the same and the fathers are usually classified higher (Rudd, 'The educational qualifications and social class of the parents of undergraduates entering British universities in 1984').

We might also ask the question 'Why do applicants from higher social backgrounds have better A-level scores?' You might think the answer is that people from the upper social groups are more likely to go to independent schools where they would receive better tuition. But I know of no evidence that the tuition is better. It is true that the A-level scores of applicants to university from independent schools are very marginally better than those from comprehensive schools, but the differences are not big enough to explain the proportions of different social groups in universities.

The most likely explanation is that the spoken language of upper social groups is closer to academic language than the speech of lower social groups. The language candidates are expected to use in written examinations comes more easily to children of parents in white-collar occupations. For children from working-class origins, academic work is more like working in a foreign language. It is more difficult. That may be one reason why these students do better in science, engineering and mathematical subjects than in arts and humanities where the use of English is more important. It is not only that academic language uses a large vocabulary. The construction of sentences is far more complex. It uses more subordinate clauses.

Do students have a particular type of personality?

No, but certain personality types do better in examinations and are therefore more likely to be selected. People who work hard are more likely to be selected. Students need to be able to work on their own. That favours applicants who are self-motivated and slightly introverted. Those who are self-motivated may be anxious to avoid failure or to achieve great things.

That's an important difference. A student who is motivated to avoid failure will do the bare minimum to get by. Those who are motivated to achieve great things are more likely to work long hours. When at school, working long hours is likely to pay off. These people do well in examinations at school and are likely to obtain places in higher education. They don't always do so well when they reach higher education. Depending on the subject they are studying, they may need to develop a new aspect to their personality.

This aspect has to do with the tolerance of uncertainty and attitudes to authority. Look at the ten characteristics listed on the left below. They often tend to go together. So do those listed on the right.

Wants certainty	Tolerates uncertainty
Accepts the authority of teachers and other experts	Independently minded
Can be conformist	Can be rebellious
Confines study to what is in the syllabus	Reads around his/her subject
Systematic and thorough learning of ground work	Explores subject wherever curiosity leads
Builds his/her knowledge upon previous knowledge	Hops from one topic to another
Wants rules or principles to apply	Challenges rules and principles
Memory and calculation are particularly important in study	Uses very varied patterns of thought. Links ideas unconventionally. Questioning mind
Has fixed patterns of thought	Tries out new ideas; innovation
Sometimes dogmatic	Sometimes accepts rules only provisionally

I am not saying that one set of characteristics tends to be good and the other bad. That depends what the student is trying to do. On the whole, the characteristics listed on the left are more frequent among science and engineering students. Those listed on the right occur more often among students of arts and humanities.

During their time in higher education, there is a tendency for students to become a bit more like the list on the right and a bit less like the list on the left. Students often start with a rather black and white view of knowledge as something dispensed by authorities which students need to accumulate. Later on, they come to accept diversity of opinions as a temporary uncertainty until authorities find out the answer. After realising that uncertainty is legitimate and very common, students may go through a stage of believing all knowledge and values are contextual and relative. It is thought that the most able students then go through progressive stages of commitment and responsibility in order to have a purpose when everything seems relative.

So it seems that, although higher education wants students of all personality types, higher education itself develops certain aspects of personality more than others.

Why do we have students from overseas?

You might ask the question: Why should we accept students from overseas into higher education? Don't they use British resources? Don't they keep some of our students out? Aren't the British subsidising other countries?

The answer is that Britain benefits politically, economically and educationally. If students coming here from overseas are treated well they return to positions of influence and can exert goodwill towards Britain which can be priceless. Furthermore, they promote democratic values and British values in particular. Educationally, Britain benefits because it attracts the best brains from other countries. Higher education benefits from an international perspective in the process of scholarship. Overseas students contribute significantly to our research output, and there are reciprocal benefits from British scholars going overseas. Economically, it can be argued that overseas students, like tourists, bring foreign currency. Their fees improve our balance of payments, and the cultural and commercial contacts made by overseas students result in future exports of British goods and services. Furthermore, it may be argued that Britain has formal obligations in treaties, cultural exchange agreements and pledges in international schemes of co-operation. In any case, there is general British support for assisting developing countries and encouraging other countries to be educationally dependent upon Britain. In particular, Britain gains enormous benefit and influence as a result of English becoming the international language. French could become the lingua franca again without the international influence of our overseas students.

Some of these reasons are intangible and difficult to quantify; and some of the benefits are very long term; but none the less, taken overall, the reasons are very powerful. The education of British students would be very much poorer without their ready contact with people from other countries.

However, there are counter-arguments. It might be said that the research carried out by overseas students is not always beneficial to Britain and, if it was, there are plenty of British students who could do it. Although there is a general correlation between the number of students from a given country and the amount of trade we do with that country, there is no reason to suppose that one is a cause of the other. Since many overseas students come from poor countries, their contribution to our balance of payments may not be massive.

However, in the long run, these quantitative and economic arguments do not weigh very heavily with me. My belief is a moral one: international co-operation is a good thing. I can't quantify its benefits, but I can tell you this: lack of international co-operation is very expensive indeed!

From whom would higher education like more applications?

Working-class, mature and overseas students

From groups that are under-represented. Six sections of society are notably under-represented in higher education, not only in Britain, but in most countries of the world: working-class, mature and overseas students, women, racial minorities and the disabled. The first three I have already considered.

Women

Forty-nine per cent of the 18-year-old population are women. Only 44 per cent of students are women, but that figure has been rising steadily for twenty years. The message of equal opportunities is slowly getting through, but we should ask where the message of unequal opportunities comes from.

It seems likely that parents, schools, friends and acquaintances set expectations and young people's self-perceptions of their roles. Particularly during adolescence and young adulthood people seek to answer the questions such as 'How do I fit in?', 'What group should I belong to?', 'What am I good at?' and 'What am I going to be?' Without some answers to these questions anyone would lack self-confidence. It only requires a stranger to remark that not many girls do engineering, for a 13-year-old girl to prefer English. And it only takes a few mates at school to want to start earning a wage, for an educationally disenchanted working-class lad to leave school at 16, whatever his intellectual ability.

Ethnic minorities

People from these under-represented groups do not apply to enter higher education because there is a mismatch between their image of themselves and their impression of what students are like. They see colleges and universities as remote institutions attended by white, middle-class, young men who were successful at school and are without family ties. They cannot see themselves as students, let alone wearing an academic gown at a graduation ceremony. They see themselves as having failed at school and likely to fail if they went to college. Most of all they have no knowledge of the educational system and don't see it as offering an investment for the future.

These impressions are particularly strong among Asian women. Asian women are usually part of an extended family in which they cannot easily decide for themselves what they will do. Asian men have much more independence, more confidence and a better knowledge of the educational system.

Afro-Caribbeans are more inclined to see the system as white-dominated and loaded against them.

Disabled

The disabled pose financial and moral problems. First, institutions cannot afford the building alterations they are legally obliged to make. That problem is particularly acute in polytechnics and the Central Institutions of Scotland, many of which have old buildings where lifts, ramps and toilets for wheelchairs are difficult to install. Second, handicapped applicants often pose borderline problems for admissions tutors. For example, should blind or deaf applicants be admitted to courses for teacher training for the sake of their own fulfilment, if they might never take a teaching post? How important is the applicant's vocational intention? Does it make a difference if he or she is keeping another person out? Is academic merit the only criterion? We all believe in equal opportunities, but, accepting that people's talents are not equal, what opportunities should there be? What special provision should be made for handicapped students? To what lengths should each institution go?

The demand for higher education has long outstripped supply. Consequently institutions have never had to woo these groups. Demand still outstrips supply, but the moral and financial pressures upon them to market higher education to these groups is growing. Questions of supply and demand on the one hand, and these moral obligations on the other, have to be seen in the context of a wider question of national policy: 'How many people should have access to higher education?'

How many people should have access to higher education?

It depends on what higher education is for – the question we asked in Chapter 2. Yet the question tends to be answered purely in terms of what employers need – occupational skills. But that is only one of the five main purposes of higher education discussed in that chapter. If you look at how people spend their lives, working hours are getting shorter. Most of people's waking hours are now spent looking at television, bringing up children, doing domestic chores and participating in social activities.

Arguments for mass higher education

Because people without higher education do these things it is assumed that higher education is not important when doing them. That is a big mistake. Unlike the way we do our job, the way we bring up our children will be passed on from generation to generation. The effects are very far reaching. It is a difficult task and there is a lot to learn. It is a role that requires judgement, the capacity to keep learning, distinctive attitudes of tolerance and understanding, and all too often, considerable emotional adjustment! This is the stuff of higher education. They are the aims discussed in Chapter 2.

People who do not look at television with a balance of criticism are ready for indoctrination. Criticism is the essence of higher education. The more technology allows information to be packaged for easy consumption, the more important mass higher education becomes for freedom of thought and the preservation of democracy.

Just as a more complex society was made possible by the growth of literacy, so our increasingly complex society, technology, legislation and Europeanisation all require ordinary citizens to exercise more judgement, to know how to find out and to be constantly learning new things. These skills are required in the home and in leisure as much as at work. Consider, for example, the legal, accountancy and social skills you need to organise a club for your favourite sport.

These are arguments for a greatly expanded higher education, to do with the nature of life, democracy and leisure. The arguments are necessarily general and may therefore seem vague, but they are crucial to the way we live.

Factors influencing government policy

Throughout the 1980s they were arguments that the government rejected as idealist and too expensive. But in 1989, after a decade of cutting back on higher education, the Minister announced the need to double provision in the following 25 years. So what factors influence its policies?

From the government's point of view, this question is seen in the context of how much spending money it should give to the UFC and the PCFC. The amount of money depends on how many people it decides should have a higher education. That decision depends on demand, first from students wanting to get in, and second from employers wanting graduates. As we saw in Chapter 2, forecasting student demand is easier than manpower planning. Let's look at seven assumptions about future demand.

The demographic downturn

First, the government's forecasts of the number of students entering higher education are based on the number of 18-year-olds that there will be until the year 2000. The number falls from 1989 until 1995, whereupon it rises until 1999 and then begins to decline again. This was used as an argument for cutback. But we have seen that higher education recruits mostly from social classes I and II. Their numbers will not decline in that way. Furthermore there was a low birth rate during the Second World War, but that did not stop demand for higher education growing rapidly eighteen years later. The hypothesis that demand reflects the number of 18-year-olds is suspect.

We have seen that the hypothesis is also suspect when it assumes that there is a limited pool of ability that institutions have reliably drained dry.

Staying-on rates

Second, demand corresponds much more closely with the number of 16-year-olds who stay on in full-time education and that reflects the willingness of schools and colleges to take them. The schools and colleges will want to keep their numbers up. Their income depends upon it. So there is little prospect of fewer young people taking A levels when the number of 18-year-olds drops. This is shown by the fact that the proportion of 16-year-olds staying on in full-time education has increased since the number of 16-year-olds began to fall in 1981. Nevertheless, that proportion (53 per cent) is lower than any other country in Western Europe except Greece. In the

Netherlands and Denmark it is over 90 per cent. So there is the potential to expand.

The age participation rate (APR)

The demand for higher education reflects how desirable it is seen to be. Desirability will affect the proportion of 18-year-olds taking higher education. This proportion is called the Age Participation Rate (APR). In 1987 it was about 14 per cent. The government then made two sets of guesses on how the APR will change by the year 2000, one that it would increase to just under 16 per cent and the other to about 18.5 per cent. These are low and high projections of demand. They expected that demand will be somewhere between the two, but if access is to double in the next 25 years many more young people will need to take A levels, the APR for social classes III, IV and V would need to approach the present rate for classes I and II, female participation should equal that for men, vocationally qualified applicants will need to increase, and there will need to be double the number of mature entrants. Even then, the British APR would be lower than the present APR for USA, Japan and most European countries. In the USA the APR has been over 50 per cent for some years.

Mature students

A fourth factor is the proportion of mature students that may seek higher education. The government distinguishes between those aged 21 to 24, over half of whom have A-level entry qualifications, and those of age 25 and over, most of whom do not have A-level qualifications. The government believed that demand from mature students would rise until 1989, would level off for five years and then begin to decline. This decline is again based upon the fact that there will be fewer people in their twenties during the second half of the 1990s, but, as we have seen, that factor can be over-emphasised. The number of young mature entrants (21 to 24 years) increased 9 per cent in the decade 1979–89, but the number of older mature entrants increased by 34 per cent. This difference has to be explained by social factors, not birth rates.

Increasing overseas students

A fifth set of assumptions concerns the numbers of students from abroad. In 1985, there were about 50,000. The government believed this might rise to about 57,000 by the year 2000, but there were already 55,600 by 1987. So surely the government has underestimated the rate of increase.

Growing part-time numbers

A sixth set of assumptions concerns the number of part-time students. The government and higher education institutions are busily encouraging an increase in the number of part-time students. On its lower projection in 1985, the government believed that their number would increase gently until 1991 and then decline in a steepening curve. Their most optimistic projection supposed a much steeper increase from 330,000 to nearly 370,000 by 1996, followed by quite a steep decline. These figures included 77,000 Open University students and 48,000 postgraduates. However there were already 359,000 part-time students in higher education by 1987, so once again the government underestimated the strength of demand.

Indeed policy makers have consistently underestimated the suppressed demand for part-time education for 200 years. People want it but they are prevented from getting it for various reasons. For example, their jobs leave little time for study, they can't afford it, they have family commitments, travel at night is too difficult, they fear failure, they fear they will not fit in with other students, or they are too tired to learn once other duties are done.

The latent demand is there. The task is to release it. For example, distance learning overcame some of these difficulties and released an unsuspected latent demand when the Open University opened in 1970.

The needs of employers

While there is no doubt that government support for higher education is strongly influenced by the demands of employers, there is no assurance that either government support or employer demand influences the number of applications. Both have sought an increase in the number of trained engineers, but they have repeatedly failed to attract the number required. At the end of the 1980s, the commercial sector recruited more graduates than the whole of British industry.

Changes needed in what higher education supplies

Government, universities, colleges and polytechnics alike now recognise the need to expand higher education. The falling number of 18-year-olds does not mean that fewer people need to be educated. It means that more technology is needed to do the jobs previously done by people; and more technology requires a more educated labour force to deal with it.

We have seen that Britain has untapped human resources it cannot afford to ignore. Its Age Participation Rate (APR) is low compared with other developed nations. A growing number of mature adults seek higher education, particularly women returning when their children no longer require their full-time attention. There is a massive part-time market if the right kind of higher education were to be provided – and that's the point.

Higher education institutions must adapt by providing what the customer wants and should select students in, not out. That is to say, they should find ways to include new groups of students rather than constantly operate a student selection process to filter and exclude. This means that institutions must do market research and change what they provide accordingly. It may well mean that higher education must:

- provide many more short courses and part-time courses;
- develop short modules that can be accumulated to gain academic awards;
- remove the stigma of failure by encouraging dropping in and dropping out;
- take courses to factories and other outside centres rather than always expecting students to come to the college;
- assess prior experiential learning (APEL) to select students;
- develop activities and learning methods suitable for mature students and others with experience to relate; and
- devise more consultancy and courses with professional groups for professional groups.

97

In short, what is needed is more 'continuing education' and higher education needs to be seen as part of it, rather than something separate that happens to be organised by a department in the same institution.

The credit accumulation and transfer schemes

One of the things that has been wrong with courses in higher education for a very long time, is that once a student has enrolled for a course, he is stuck with it for a period of three or four years. If he moves to another district or leaves for some other reason he gets no credit for what he has done. In effect higher education has presented a rather take-it-or-leave-it attitude. Student applicants must hunt for the course that suits their needs best and if they are not accepted where they want to go, or if there is nothing to suit their particular needs, they must put up with something they don't really want.

We have also recognised that as courses become more vocationally orientated, people with work experience should be given some credit for what they have learnt on the job (APEL), instead of all credit being based upon certificates obtained by taking academic examinations. There needs to be some way of giving academic credit for work experience so that people who have that experience can take shorter courses.

In effect what has existed for so long is a range of three- or four-year menus with no option but to choose one of them, or none of them. What is needed is to allow students to take dishes from several of the fixed menus and leave with credit for what they have done without taking a full three-year meal.

The solution to these two problems is to devise a system that gives credit to a student who has taken selected units of a course or who has work experience from which he or she will have gained equivalent learning. Credit given by one institution must be recognised by another and by employers. In other words the credit must be transferable from one educational institution to another.

The scheme being devised by the CNAA is called the Credit Accumulation Transfer Scheme (CATS). This scheme allows students to qualify for awards of the CNAA and some universities by putting together units of courses from a number of different institutions or other sources. The pattern of attendance (including non-attendance) at those institutions may vary. Where credit is given for formal courses of study or learning gained by experience, awards are obtained by accumulating between 4 and 120 credit points for a successfully completed course unit. One hundred and twenty credit points is equivalent to a one-year full-time course for a normal student.

The CNAA is operating the CATS scheme at both undergraduate and postgraduate levels. To obtain a degree the student's overall programme of study must demonstrate coherence, balance and progression. That is to say a student cannot acquire tit-bits of knowledge here and there and expect that, say, 360 units will give him a degree. Without being tied to traditional degree courses, the units must nonetheless hang together and some units must be more advanced in the sense that their successful completion depends upon knowledge and abilities recognised in less advanced units. You cannot get a degree if all the units are at an elementary level. Course units passed and the grades obtained on them are listed on a transcript and a record kept at the CNAA headquarters. The grades are assigned by examiners on a sixteen-point scale between 0 (fail) and 16 (excellent). Course units are assigned to three levels. Level 1 is called Certificate level. Level 2 is equivalent to a Diploma of Higher Education, a two-year post-A-level course. Level 3 is degree level; but you will only get a degree if you have above average grade points on a majority of level 3 units, normally passed at the first attempt.

Indeed this option may be preferable for students taking units at a large number of different institutions. The Council operates a personal advisory service at their London headquarters. The Council will give a credit rating for the qualifications and experience a student applicant already possesses and this may strengthen his chances of admission to programmes of study offered by polytechnics or other institutions. This advisory service is only available to those wanting unusual courses of study or having unusual qualifications. Applicants within the normal range will be referred to other careers and guidance services.

No transfer scheme will work if institutions do not recognise the value of each other's courses. To get every institution to agree to everything all at once is asking a bit much. So the scheme has begun by groups making agreements and operating the scheme between themselves. These groups are of two kinds. One is groups of institutions within a region. The other is groups of academics within related academic fields. The hope is that these networks will gradually grow until everyone is involved.

The scheme is of particular interest to employers who train their own employees. Up till now employees have received no recognition outside their company for training they have received within it. The CATS scheme will make their training more marketable so that they can apply for jobs elsewhere. You might think that this would discourage employers from being involved because they would constantly be losing their newly trained staff. But that is not the case. The CATS scheme makes training more attractive and therefore helps to improve the quality of their workforce. Furthermore when they receive applications from staff in other companies the transcript gives a better indication of the training they have received than the labels attached to many academic courses.

Conclusion

In this chapter we looked first at the present procedures for selecting students and the consequences of those procedures, the kind of students we get. We then turned our attention to the kind of students we don't get enough of – women, working-class, racial minorities, the disabled and older people.

That raised policy questions about access to higher education. In particular, how can the number of students be increased. The answer to that question depends on what higher education can supply. Simply to supply more of the traditional three- and four-year degree courses will not do. Higher education needs an alternative model, the model of continuing education. Universities, colleges and polytechnics need to organise activities that relate students' experience and give credit for it. They also need to let students shop around and accumulate credit for learning acquired in different places.

Thus questions to do with access are at the forefront of change in higher education.

Further reading

Sir Christopher Ball, *Aim Higher – widening access to higher education* (Royal Society of Arts, 1989).
Ernest Rudd, 'The educational qualifications and social class of the parents of undergraduates entering British universities in 1984', *The Journal of the Royal Statistical Society* (1987).

Chapter 7

WAYS OF LEARNING

A student's job is to learn. But how? All students arrive with some skills in how to learn, but they're not always appropriate. This chapter looks at why. It tries to give an understanding of what is required and why some students find learning easier than others. The way students learn depends partly on their schooling, their temperament, and how they were brought up. Every student has a different background and I can't describe them all. So I'll sketch a couple of contrasting characters. The sketches are caricatures. As caricatures, they may seem judgemental and unfairly critical. They're not supposed to be. Indeed, the message I want to get across is the need to be understanding.

Understanding why students behave as they do

The two students are Kim and Robin. People called Kim are just as often male as female, and Robins, though more often male, are sometimes female, but it is easier to distinguish one from the other if I write as if they are of different sexes. Kim is a little dependent and conformist, while Robin is more independent.

Kim had a conventional middle-class upbringing. She is quiet and conscientious. Her parents are not reckless, spontaneous or humorous and in personal relations they are a little tense and a bit formal. Kim is a product of the Protestant ethic: she works hard and does not spend money freely because she is not given much by her parents. She has not been told to go to church regularly. She does so because that is the thing to do. She has accompanied her family to church for as long as she can remember. Since before she first went to school, her parents and her church have provided a consistent moral authority. Matters of right and wrong are not open matters. They have correct answers. Reference to the Bible, convention, parents or other established authorities provides guidance when an individual is uncertain. But there is no uncertainty in reality; all is clear so long as you know.

Unlike Kim, Robin experienced inconsistent values. When, before the age of 5, he did something wrong in the morning, Mum would threaten that Dad would tan his backside when he came home that evening. But if Robin was a good boy in the afternoon, Mum would forget about that. So what his parents said was not consistent. The rules were varying all the time. Because one day was different from another, Robin soon learnt to be constantly testing to find out what he could get away with. So Robin learnt to be an opportunist. He acquired quick judgement in sizing up a situation. His behaviour was governed less by rules, than by expediency and what was practical at the time.

Experience at school

It was the same when they went to school. Kim soon discovered that all the authorities agreed. Both her parents, the teachers and the textbooks all agreed about what was true and what was not true. Her job was to learn it. So learning was a process of collecting facts and memorising them. For this she was well rewarded with adult approval. Basically, Kim had a very secure environment and people were tender-hearted towards her.

Robin's experience was very different. He continually created situations in which power had to be exerted. Every teacher has met Robin. He was always testing the limits of the implicit rules laid down by the teachers. When the class was told to be quiet, he would whisper to his neighbour. The teacher would ignore it and Robin would feel able to whisper a little louder. This process would go on until the teacher felt his authority was being challenged. Then Robin had to be checked or punished. That meant that the relationship between Robin and his teachers was more tough than tender, more to do with compulsion than caring. He never had security. He was always being repressed and sooner or later his repressed feelings would emerge as aggression. That aggression might be expressed acceptably in sport, less acceptably in poking fun at other pupils and teachers, or unacceptably in more misbehaviour. Misbehaviour simply provoked a vicious circle with the teachers becoming more and more short tempered and punitive towards him. Robin learnt to live by his wits and by expediency because, in spite of outward appearances, he had never had a stable relationship to rely on.

However, the rules at school were more consistent than at home. Robin gradually learnt to play the school game by the school rules. True, he continued to transgress more often than Kim, and because of his reputation, he was not so easily forgiven. He continued to experience more punishments than she. Nonetheless, to a very large extent, the school provided some stability for Robin. Without it he might have tried some petty pilfering and got the wrong side of the law.

Robin progressed academically because he feared failure and punishment; while Kim progressed because she tried to do her best all the time. Robin tried to minimise failure. Kim tried to maximise achievement. So Robin did as little as possible to get by. You might think that, in contrast, Kim went beyond the call of duty, but she soon learnt that that was a mistake.

Psychologically speaking, enterprise in learning was punished. When she showed initiative and produced ideas and information with which her teachers were not familiar, they felt insecure. For example, when learning about ants, she discovered from an encyclopaedia at home that ants have an enemy that sprays acid at them. On volunteering this information in class, the biology teacher reacted with mild aggression by questioning her more deeply, saying 'What do you know about that?' and 'You don't need to know about that yet'. The teacher felt threatened because he had only prepared a lesson on ants, not on their enemies.

Restricting her knowledge to that prescribed by those with power over her threatened no one in authority, and all were rewarded with the security that comes from not considering awkward questions. Limiting her memory to the facts prescribed by the teachers was always adequate to gain high marks and to earn the warm approval of both teachers and her parents. Education was a process of memorising the established facts and regurgitating them when required, particularly in examinations and tests.

Unlike Kim, Robin found that the easiest way to get by was not to sit down and try to remember all the facts in splendid isolation, but to try to understand how they were linked together. So although Robin learnt less, he understood it better. At first, understanding and connecting one thing with another was not rewarded very much, but as he worked his way up the secondary school, this learning strategy began to pay off.

So it was that, although pupils like Robin are the scourge of their teachers when lower down the school and those without much ability leave at the age of 16, those with some ability obtain GCSEs good enough to enter the sixth form. Robin was made a school prefect, partly because it was expedient for the teachers to have him on their side in the war against indiscipline; and partly because he played rugby well and that was seen as leadership.

Kim was not regarded by her teachers as unimaginative and having no other interests than her school work because she sang in the school choir and was a member of the Christian Union. In the choir, she learnt to sing a fraction of a second after everyone else so that if she made a mistake it would not be noticed. In the Christian Union, she learnt to observe discussions without ever actually taking part. She thereby safely avoided any need to justify an opinion. This masterly avoidance of anything controversial, or of making any contribution at all, was later so well developed for use in university seminars, that she was in danger of becoming conspicuously inconspicuous.

Because she was conscientious, did her best and did as she was told, Kim was regarded as a sound, but not outstanding, pupil academically. Because she never caused any trouble, her teachers steadily came to regard her as a good pupil. Good pupils are likely to succeed and success meant eventually going to college as they had done. Indeed the expectation of higher education had unwittingly been planted in her mind by the age of 13 or 14.

Because of the limitations of the school timetable, it was at

that age that both she and Robin found it necessary to special-
ise in some subjects. Now pupils like Kim are less likely to
opt for science subjects than languages, humanities and the
social sciences because it may be beyond the ability of a conscientious pupil to do well in mathematics, but a conscientious
pupil will always get reasonable marks in arts subjects, such
as history, geography and English. So when her parents looked
at her end of term reports, the prospect of sixth-form studies in
pure and applied mathematics, physics and computing looked
unwise. On the other hand, Robin, never one to sit over books
for a long time, much preferred practical classes in science.

When they reached the sixth form, both Kim and Robin
worked very hard, under pressure from both their teachers
and their parents, to get good enough grades to enter higher
education. Entry is highly competitive.

The experience of higher education

When he arrived at college, Robin experienced the 'decompression syndrome'. His previous life had consisted almost
entirely of two social worlds: school and home. Suddenly, in a
matter of weeks, both these were removed. Gone were the
pressures to conform. Gone were the pressures to work. He
had achieved his recent goals to pass A levels and enter higher
education. He had not yet acquired new ones. His parents were
no longer there to insist that he did his homework before doing
other things. In his first week, the Freshers' week, all the
clubs and societies of the Students' Union put on displays to
tempt him to join. He joined five, one for each weekday evening, and on Saturday, there was sport in the afternoon and a
disco in the evening. On Saturday and Sunday mornings, he
tended to sleep in so that the remainder of Sunday was the
only time when he could work without feeling that in a short
while he must get up and go to some other activity. In fact his
first week at college set his life-style for most of the next three
years.

At first, it didn't seem to matter very much. The lecturers
were not asking him to hand in work tomorrow. Because the
syllabuses of the various A-level examining boards were different, some of the first-year courses repeated work he had done

at school. With his self-confident extrovert nature and his ability to think quickly on his feet, he was quite vocal in tutorials and only his most experienced tutors realised that he was not doing much work.

For Kim, it was different. She did not experience decompression because she kept the pressure on herself. She was self-disciplined. Her conscience was well developed. However, because her teachers had not given her homework to be handed in next week, she was not certain exactly what to do. One tutor had not told her anything; another had given her a bibliography a page long and she didn't know where to start. At school, she only had four books in that subject and they lasted the whole year. With the guidance of the teacher, she had worked steadily through them gathering information and noting them as she went. She realised that at college she would not have the close supervision of her teachers. At college, you have to be more independent, but she assumed that independence meant doing the same thing without the close supervision. After all, that is the way she had been taught to study. Taking notes from lectures was much the same. At school, she was given guidance in what to note; notes were sometimes virtually dictated. She saw that she now had the responsibility to select what she noted. This made her a little anxious because she might miss some important item of knowledge. The obvious thing was to play it safe and note as much as she could. As the weeks passed, her files of notes grew steadily thicker and she eyed them with a sense of achievement. For there, in those folders, was her knowledge.

Kim never discussed her work with other students. Why should she? She never did at school; in fact, talking in class was strongly discouraged there, and when else could you talk about your work? It was the same at college: 'You shouldn't talk in lectures and it's difficult in the library.' Her friends on the same corridor in the hall of residence did not take the same subject. She met people taking the same course in her department, but there was neither time nor place there to permit lengthy or profound discussion. For a long time, Kim didn't realise that discussion is an important part of student life. She thought discussion simply wasted time better spent in reading. After all, she had heard someone say that she was 'reading' for a degree.

Robin, on the other hand, went to the Union bar both at lunch-time and in the evening. There he would talk about all manner of subjects with students from many different disciplines. He developed opinions about society and politics as well as discussing wide-ranging scientific and cultural issues that set his honours course in a wider context. Robin was getting quite a different kind of education. He was getting through a number of girl friends, and he was also getting addicted to alcohol. In later life, this damaged his liver and made him put on weight, but, for the moment, it showed more in his bank balance than his health and he worked some of it off in his sporting life.

Paradoxically, the personality characteristics of both Kim and Robin favour the subjects they chose not to do at the age of 13. Kim's conformity is quite acceptable in science, medicine and engineering; while, at the Union bar, Robin acquired the breadth, independence and argumentative skill that is advantageous in the arts and social sciences.

Implications for academic style and academic work

It is the purpose of higher education to change people, or more precisely, for them to change themselves. So if Kim and Robin were to stay as they were when they arrived, their higher education would have failed.

If students like Kim don't develop more independence of mind, they get low marks for their assignments, become anxious and depressed, try to work yet harder, and then overwork so that their minds become dulled rather than sparkling. In short, they get in a vicious circle of low academic confidence, overwork and excessive fatigue, leading to poor performance and even less academic confidence. If it is the purpose of higher education to broaden their outlook, to encourage original thinking, to challenge traditional beliefs, to practise the arts of criticism, to provide a meeting of lively minds . . . students like Kim have a long way to develop when they first arrive at college. When Kim first arrived, she didn't have a lively mind; and she sought the security of a few like-minded friends. She was unconsciously afraid that originality would disturb the values, relationships and support of her family and throw an unwanted and unaccustomed spotlight on her private thoughts.

That is not to say that Kim didn't have some very fine qualities when she first arrived in higher education. She was very reliable, hard working and unambitious. She was scrupulously honest. She would not object to monotonous tasks and any company that might have employed her would have got good value for low wages. But in higher education those qualities are not enough.

In practice most students like Kim do use their time in higher education to explore ideas, values and personalities they would not have experienced at home. If, during her second year, you see Kim untidily dressed with her arm slung round the waist of the long-haired drummer of a college pop group, perhaps you should sigh with satisfaction that she is growing up normally.

If, in his first year, Robin does not learn to take more responsibility, to organise himself and plan his use of time, to use the academic as well as the social resources of his institution, to heed his longer-term priorities and to discipline himself to concentrate at his desk, he may fail his first-year exams and drop out of college altogether. Compared with other students, he has always taken risks and lived for the present; but higher education is a long-term investment. He needs to recognise that the risks are greater now and there is not always someone at hand to protect him from his lack of self-discipline.

That is not to say that Robin's first year would have been wasted if he had dropped out. That is a common misconception and can give an unnecessary sense of failure. He matured a great deal in the Students' Union. His interpersonal and social skills, his numerical competence and scientific background, his confidence and energy, his powers of communication and quick thinking, have all been further developed. To these qualities he has added some experience of organising Union events, a broader understanding of other people and an ability to defend his own point of view. Many a company, particularly

109

in business and commerce, would value these qualities and his energy.

It is a great mistake to think that the only benefits of higher education are academic and the piece of paper at the end; and it is a great injustice to stigmatise those who have the courage to change their minds in the first year, and decide to do something different. We need to encourage more people to get some of what higher education has to offer, without using three years' worth of resources.

On the whole, higher education and the students in it are successful. Only 13 per cent drop out. Students like Kim and Robin change a great deal. The degree result that Robin gets will depend on the strength of his motivation and the quality of his study methods. If Kim is to perform well in arts, humanities or the social sciences, she will need to develop more confidence and independence of mind; but, with that proviso, her ability is likely to be the most important factor influencing the class of degree she gets because, whatever subject she takes, she will always try her very best.

Nevertheless, academic success, like many things worthwhile, is often only achieved after a struggle. The struggle not only gives the student some anxiety, but the parents as well, not least because they cannot do much about it. Their children are leaving the nest and must fly for themselves. Take comfort. The best academics struggle for excellence too. It's normal.

At college the first three weeks are crucial. It is during that time that students establish their new lifestyle. Changes after that are more difficult. Their new responsibilities are both domestic and academic. They must adjust to the demands of their new residence and the college timetable. They will need to learn to organise their time, to study and learn in new ways, and to make new friends. The rest of this chapter aims to give some tips on these things.

Planning the use of time

The first thing for students to do is to monitor their use of time. I recommend the following exercise which I have used with hundreds of students. Draw up at least seven sheets of A4 paper, one for each day of the week, in the manner shown

Hour	10	20	30	40	50	Hour
6 a.m.						
7 a.m.						
8 a.m.						
9 a.m.						
10 a.m.						
11 a.m.						
12 a.m.						
1 p.m.						
2 p.m.						
3 p.m.						
4 p.m.						
5 p.m.						
6 p.m.						
7 p.m.						
8 p.m.						
9 p.m.						
10 p.m.						
11 p.m.						
12 a.m.						
1 a.m.						
2 a.m.						

Figure 7.1 Sheet for students to monitor the use of their time

in Figure 7.1. Ten-minute blocks of time are marked off between the hours of 6 a.m. and 2 a.m. It assumes that students are asleep between the hours of 3 a.m. and 6 a.m. (That may be an optimistic assumption for some Robins.) At the end of each day, and emphatically no later because otherwise he will forget, the student should place an initial letter indicating the predominant activity in that ten-minute period. (When I give the instructions students often think every ten minutes is too frequent, but in practice it is a convenient unit. They quickly block off long periods of time, such as for sleep and practical classes, without repeatedly writing S or P. Using longer units results in significant activities, such as journeys on campus, not being represented.)

I have found that the following classification works very well, but there is nothing to stop students adopting their own if they wish.

L   Lectures and other formal class teaching
G   Group discussion, formal seminars, tutorials, group teaching
P   Practicals, fieldwork, laboratory work organised by teachers
O   Other academic work, including private studying
X   Extra-mural activities, organised recreation, clubs and socie-
    ties, attendance at church, concerts, theatre, dances, cinema
I   Informal recreation, having coffee with friends, visiting
    another's residence, 'chatting with friends', informal discussion
D   Domestic activities. Getting dressed, having a bath, cooking,
    eating, cleaning, shopping, any activity essential to life not
    classified elsewhere
T   Travel. To and from work, walking between departments, travel
    for shopping, to and from organised extra-mural activities (X)
S   Sleep, including rest during the day
M   Miscellaneous, including time spent filling in the chart

You will see that there are ten items. Apart from 'Miscel-laneous' they are in three groups: Work, Recreation and Necessities of life. Call them W, R and N, if you like.

Of course the amounts of time spent in different kinds of work will vary with the subject of study. While engineers may spend twelve hours a week in practical work, arts students may spend none. Social work and management students may spend a lot of time in group discussion and little in lectures. On the other hand the averages for recreation and necessities in my researches, shown in Figure 7.2, have been remarkably consistent. But they are only averages. Averages hide the variations between individuals. Furthermore averages don't tell us how long students ought to spend doing each of these things.

Nonetheless if a student's life-style is very different from other students' he should at least look to see whether he is

W = 38 hours	L	8
	G	2
	P	5
	O	23
R = 36 hours	X	16
	I	20
N = 91 hours	D	20
	T	10
	S	61
	M	3

Figure 7.2 Average lengths of time spent by arts and engineering students

spending his time wisely. If Robin spends less than 30 hours a week at work, he should write out a list of the tasks he ought to carry out and log them in a written plan of how he is going to spend his time in the coming week. He will say that this particular week was exceptional, but every week is exceptional in higher education. It is important to work steadily, not irregularly, to get the best out of it.

If Kim works over 52 hours a week her brain is probably too tired to be efficient. Yet she probably feels that if she works less, she won't get the work done. She may need counselling and her tutor's understanding to have the confidence to rest and relax, before she discovers that she can do as much in less time when she is fresh.

Here is a convenient rule of thumb about the use of private study time (O). For every hour of lectures students spend nearly the same amount of time looking over their lecture notes – basically learning the facts taught in the lecture (Total = 2L). The preparation time for group discussions varies a great deal; it may be about four times the group discussion time (Total = 5G). Although students have to write up their practical workbooks, compared with the length of the practicals themselves, the time taken is small; so I shall count it as zero. The remainder of other work time is available to the student as 'personal thinking time' to read around the subject, to go beyond the tasks set by the teachers, to develop ideas of his own, to explore academic interests, and generally 'to develop the powers of the mind' as discussed in Chapter 2.

Now there is a curious fact. It seems that no matter how much or how little time is spent in lectures, group discussions and practicals, the average time spent on work is the same (around 38 hours). It is other work time (O) that changes with changes in timetabling. So typically the amount of 'personal thinking time' students have is

38 hours minus (2L plus 5G plus P) hours

Using the data I have given above that would be:

38 hours minus (16 plus 10 plus 5) hours = 7 hours

In many subjects the amount that students think on their own has a strong influence on their success. It also leads to a curious conclusion that has been confirmed by experiment: up to a point, if the teachers teach less, students do better because they have time to think more about what they have been taught.

Effective reading

Many people say they read slowly when they don't. Nevertheless, students like Kim were unwittingly taught, or taught themselves, to study everything slowly and thoroughly. At college there simply isn't time for that strategy. In most subjects it is more important to know how to scan a text quickly. (There are important exceptions. In quantitative and science subjects, for example, one must follow each step of important calculations or procedures.)

Let us imagine Kim, who has to read up on a topic before writing an essay or attending a seminar. Very likely the tutor has recommended a reading list far longer than any human being could manage in the time, because if he only gave a short list the first students to arrive in the library would borrow the only copies available and prevent others from reading them until the seminar is over. She should consult the author and subject catalogues in the library to find out where to go. Very often they are listed on a computer.

When consulting any book on the shelves there are up to

four stages she may go through. After any one of these stages she may put the book back on the shelf if she judges that it will no longer merit any further time for her present purpose.

The preview

The first stage is the preview. At this stage she should ask herself 'Is this book of any interest?', 'How does it relate to the topic of the essay or seminar?' To answer those questions she should look at the title, the dust cover and the index. Students often neglect the index, but used intelligently it can direct them to the precise pages required and save a great deal of time.

The overview

The second stage is the overview. At this stage she should ask, 'How does the author see the subject?', 'What does he include and what issues does he not consider?' She should already have an indication of the answers to the latter question from having read the dust cover and contents at the preview stage. But she can get more detail by turning to the Preface, the Conclusion or the Introduction where the author summarises his viewpoint. If the book has more than seven chapters it is useful to try to put them into less than seven groups in order to see the structure of the book and the major questions that the author has asked himself when dividing up the subject matter. It is a matter of understanding the way the author thinks. Look at the Contents section of this book and try it for yourself (but if you're really smart you will have noticed how I grouped the chapters at the end of the introductory chapter – Chapter 1). Many students fail to read the Preface of a book because they think that all the facts are to be found in the chapters. That may be; but it is not the facts that are of first importance, important as they may be, but the ideas that link them together and the most important of those may well be found in the Preface.

Kim need not read the Preface word by word from beginning to end. She should ignore those sections where the author is thanking his/her secretary (for typing), his/her wife/husband (for tolerance) and their children (without whose help it would

have been written in half the time!). She should look for the
section that says why the author wrote the book. It may be
claimed that there is a gap in the literature, or that the book
contains a particular viewpoint that has not previously been
expressed in print. It is this last point, where the author
declares any bias, that is crucial for the student to absorb.
Without that she cannot get an understanding of the book,
though she may, like Kim, memorise a lot of the facts con-
tained within it.

The flip-through

At the third stage, the flip-through, the student will take this
process a step further, asking 'What is the gist of what the
author is saying?', 'What is his/her general argument?',
'What's worth closer reading?' To do this she will use the
Index and the Contents as before, but she should also develop
skipping and skimming techniques. A useful technique when
skipping is to read the first sentence in each paragraph in
order to get a quick summary. It also helps the student to
relate one part of the book or chapter to another because her
mind does not become clouded with detail. In skimming, her
eye should pass over all the text searching for what seem to
be the important concepts. Getting and understanding the
concepts commonly used in a discipline is often the most important thing to do when first studying a subject in higher education. Discussing the theories and the facts relevant to them
comes later.

Read and test

The fourth and final stage is to read and test. It is reserved
for books, articles or chapters that justify close attention for
the student's particular purpose. She should ask herself 'Is
what the author says true, good or valid?', 'What are his
sources of evidence or the nature of his reasoning?' As always
in higher education, the student's task is as much to ask
questions, to imagine possible answers and to think of ways
to test them, as it is to know answers. She should read con-
sciously trying to relate one thing to another. And she should
note her personal reactions to what she reads. In particular

	To help at the time	For a later record
Attention	1 Concentrate	2 Evidence of attendance
Content	3 Select what's important	4 Syllabus covered
Understand structure	5 See development of topics	6 Relate and reorganise topics
Memory	7 Aids to memory	8 Revision

Figure 7.3 Why take notes?

she should note what she does not understand, rather than recording only what she does.

Note-taking

Many students are anxious about note-taking when they enter higher education, not least mature students who one might have thought would have gained note-taking experience elsewhere. For others note-taking is habitual. Lecturers will tell you that the difference between an undergraduate and a postgraduate is that if you say 'Good morning' to a class of undergraduates they say 'Good morning', while postgraduates write it down.

As you will see from Figure 7.3, there are eight reasons why students might wish to take notes. Some are to help them at the time that they write them. Others are to keep a record for later use.

Aids to concentration

Some students will say: 'I take notes to help me concentrate. It's better than chewing gum.' Lectures of an hour may be a long time to concentrate upon mathematical calculations in economics or physics. When, as often happens, the student has one lecture after another, the demands upon concentration are very great. Writing notes keeps the mind active.

Rarely as evidence of attendance

The use of notes to verify that a student has attended a course is now extremely rare in higher education, because even when attendance is obligatory, colleges would not check up in that way, even where certificates of attendance are issued.

Select what's important

Many students take notes to select the important points from a lecture, a discussion or a book. When a student has done this he may use his knowledge of the important points in several different ways.

Know the syllabus covered

In mathematics and some of the physical sciences students will use their notes as a summary of the syllabus. They may say 'I didn't understand the lecture at the time, but these notes tell me what I have to go and study in the textbooks'.

See the structure of the topic

Other students may say that the important points are like a set of headings showing how a lecturer or an author has developed a description or the steps of an argument. It helps if students know that lectures, articles and books commonly structure their subject matter in one or more of three ways.

The most common is to have headings, sub-headings and sub-sub-headings to form a hierarchy. When taking notes in these lectures students need to look out for signals about the lecture structure, such as 'Thirdly', 'Next', 'These may be divided into two types' and so on.

The second is to have a series of steps in a developmental sequence or a chain of reasoning. If a student detects this kind of structure, he needs not only to identify each of the steps, but to concentrate on the links between one step and the next. Remember a chain of argument is only as strong as its weakest link. Indeed it is interesting that lecturers often cover the blackboard with one equation after another, but they don't write verbal explanations of how one line of a calculation follows from the previous one. They often say it, but they don't write it. The lecturer may say, 'Now if we substitute this expression in that equation, we get . . .'. When attending these lectures it is important to listen for these explanations and note them too. They are often forgotten when the student gets back to his room at night, and he can spend a lot of time and exasperation working them out for himself. The trouble is that there often isn't time in a lecture to note all these things. The student must overcome this by inventing his own symbols or shorthand for words or explanations that often occur.

The third structure, and the least common, is the problem-centred presentation. It is most common in research articles or seminars, because research usually tries to answer a problem. On these occasions the student must constantly ask himself, 'What is the crux of the problem?' and then try to focus all the facts in a way that is relevant to it. Tutorial discussions may sometimes seem confused because the students have not distinguished the crucial issues. The way to unscramble a confused discussion is to note the crucial questions on different parts of a page, and then note further points under the most appropriate question. When there is only one central question, some people recommend jotting points down connected by lines so that, in the end, the notes look like a tree with a central trunk and many branches and twigs.

Relate and reorganise later study

Another student may see the key points as the framework around which to organise later study. In other words he looks for ways to relate additional points, facts, issues, ideas or concepts (call them what you like) to the key points. Particularly when using notes from lectures or a key text in this way, students need to spread them out with a clear layout on broad lined paper so that later ideas, self-directed questions and information from other sources can easily be added to the same sheet. Otherwise notes on the same topic will be all over the place on many different sheets.

A related and very important use of notes in this way is to take ideas in one section, and deliberately try to relate them to ideas dealt with in other courses or in different parts of the same course. Finding connections between things is a skill important in academic work and most walks of life. To note one's personal thoughts and reactions is an insufficiently used technique to personalise learning, but it is very effective in enhancing memory and thought about a subject. In particular it is important for students to note questions and what they do not understand. Awareness of one's own ignorance guides further study and prevents the wrong choice of exam questions.

Aids to memory

Students often fear that by noting one point in a lecture, they will miss another. However there is ample experimental evidence to show that, on balance, taking notes aids students' memories of material presented. This benefit is vastly greater if students re-read their notes the same day as they were written. Furthermore, if this is done, students can usually add points that could not be written at the time.

Revision

Most students use notes as their major source during revision. When students keep reviewing their notes throughout the year, particularly if when doing so, they try to link one part of the syllabus with another, they perform better in examinations. Similarly, those who start revising in earnest six weeks before their exams perform better than those who start only three weeks before. Too often revision is only a process of memorising rather than using information to solve problems or support arguments.

Learning from lectures

Lectures are seen as the main method of teaching in higher education; and that is a paradox. The paradox is this. A lot of research shows that lectures are mostly useful for teaching information, not for developing powerful minds, standards of culture and citizenship, or appropriate emotions, attitudes and motivation. In other words, lectures will not achieve most of the aims we considered important in Chapter 2. They are a legacy from the time when books and other sources of learning were scarce.

That explains the paradox – in higher education ways of learning are more important than ways of teaching. That is why the emphasis of this chapter is all about what the students do, not what the teachers do.

For Kim and Robin lectures are a new method of learning. Lectures have been described as periods of time during which the notes of the lecturer are transferred to the notebooks of the students without going through the brains of either. Kim and Robin have to learn how to get the best out of them.

What advice can be given? Not a lot. I gave some tips in the last section: review a lecture as soon as possible afterwards; notice the way the lecturer has organised his subject; keep trying to cross-relate the subject; note your own thoughts and reactions including what you don't understand; develop your own shorthand; and identify the crucial issues in discussion and try to relate everything to them.

There are some other tips. Lecturers often seem to talk very fast. They don't really, but they sometimes assume that students have fully understood one point when they go on to the next. The tip is to do a little reading on the topic for half an hour before the lecture so that understanding is a little easier. Obviously it is necessary to find out what the next topic will be. I am not saying that the student should study the topic thoroughly before a lecture. That would be difficult and time-consuming. It would also leave too little time for follow-up study on the last topic. I am saying do a little, primarily to grasp the basic concepts and terms in the language of the subject. For this purpose look at elementary textbooks and popular magazines like *Scientific American*. These texts will often describe the key issues in a simple manner too. They are usually too elementary for the lecturer to put on his reading list. Reading before a lecture is a matter of doing what comes easily and not feeling guilty about it. Reading after a lecture requires all the intensive skills already described in the section on 'Effective reading'.

Concentration in lectures is another problem. It is difficult for everyone. It is easier for those sitting in the middle not too far from the front. In that position the stimulus of the teacher is greater and the lecturer's non-verbal communication is much more easily perceived and interpreted, albeit often unconsciously. Attention soon wanders when the student leans back; all those who are spineless should lean forward. Excessive food, alcohol and warm rooms also make concentration difficult. Athletes and sportsmen work hard at keeping themselves in peak condition. Being an effective student increasingly requires the same dedication, but this is not yet generally recognised.

The importance of discussion

Thinking and feeling develop in discussion. That is why discussion is a crucial process in higher education. Colleges exist so that students, including academics, can talk together. Discussion provides the interaction of minds and the testing of ideas on which research depends. In this sense all students are researchers. They are, or should be, seeking the truth as they see it. Seeking the truth is a process of solving problems. Solving problems should be the focus of written work, reading and discussion.

Taking part in discussions requires a lot of skill. There are many different kinds of discussion in higher education. There's an encyclopaedia that lists over a hundred. For example, a seminar is a discussion preceded by a presentation of some kind. The presentation may be a student's essay, a talk or a literary text. Some seminars are tutorials. A tutorial is a discussion with a tutor. Tutors typically expect three to five hours' preparation for tutorials, if not the submission of written work. What the preparation is, will vary with the subject. In science and engineering it may consist of working on, though not necessarily solving, a number of problems.

For discussion in the arts, humanities and the social sciences there are seven useful steps in preparation which may each occur in the discussion itself:

- clarify terms and concepts;
- decide the major issues;
- concisely state the viewpoints of authors;

- criticise each viewpoint;
- support each viewpoint;
- make up one's own mind; and
- relate the issues to other topics and practical applications.

Confidence is necessary to get the full benefit from discussions. Students like Kim will do better if they can contribute early in a discussion. The longer they leave it, the more they feel something must have been said that renders their contribution unintelligent, and the more nervous they become. It is also a good idea to contribute early because early contributions create the framework of the discussion and it is always more difficult to contribute to another person's framework than one's own. Furthermore early contributors don't feel the same pressure to contribute later but, having broken the ice, they usually do.

Kim will get confidence when she realises that criticisms of her ideas are not criticisms of her. Indeed good ideas are those that are most worth testing. When she realises this she will be more willing to comment on other people's ideas. That is when minds begin to be stretched.

The importance of discussions can be illustrated in another way. Robin may skip lectures with impunity, but if he doesn't turn up to tutorials and seminars, questions will soon be asked. If he doesn't turn up when it is his turn to give the initial presentation, or if he turns up having not prepared anything, other students will soon let their feelings be known. (Other students will apply the pressure, not just the tutor; and that may be different from school.) Tutorials and seminars therefore combine strict deadlines with a demand for the highest quality of which the student is capable.

Surveys show that after students have left college it is discussion teaching they most remember, most appreciate and from which they learnt most.

Personal learning

Personal learning passes unnoticed. When talking of ways of learning in higher education, it is natural to concentrate upon academic learning. If asked, 'What have you learnt today?', it is very difficult to say 'I've learnt some skills of friendship. I can understand better how some people react to me. I've improved in saying "No" tactfully. I understand myself better' and so on. Yet these and a million other pieces of interpersonal learning take place in higher education. They don't appear on the syllabus and there are no examinations in them.

You may say: 'Higher education is no different from anywhere else for interpersonal learning.' The answer is yes and no. Residence and college social life create an unusual environment. Sexual relationships are particularly unusual. As one student counsellor put it, 'Where else do you sit with your girl friend, opposite your previous girl friend, every morning at breakfast?' Students are at a time of life when personal relationships are intense, rapidly changing, very public and the subject of discussion by others in a social environment from which there is no escape.

Between 6 per cent and 8 per cent of university students drop out for reasons that could be described as social and emotional. These factors affect how long and how hard students can work.

Where to get help

Student life can be very stressful. The point should not be over-emphasised; the majority of students have the time of their lives as well as working very hard. Nevertheless students (and their lecturers) suffer from more nervous illnesses, even suicides, than otherwise comparable members of the population.

Parents often find it hurtful that students no longer place them in a confidante role. Indeed a parent is often the last person a student would want to discuss personal problems with.

Many colleges allocate a personal tutor to each student. The system creates a conflicting relationship – teacher, or *in loco parentis* – and its success depends on the personal chemistry between tutor and student which cannot be guaranteed.

Most universities, polytechnics and colleges now recognise this and have a number of services to deal with these problems. First there is a student health service. Typically institutions will have one doctor for every two or three thousand students – a better ratio than for the population as a whole. Doctors soon become familiar with the kind of illnesses students present. Very often the doctors will be part-time with students so that they keep their hand in on general medicine during the rest of the week.

Virtually every institution has a counsellor nowadays, though he or she may also double as an academic member of staff. Students usually prefer someone who is wholly independent. Although counselling services are increasingly well-used, on the whole students use them too little and too late. They often mistakenly think consultation is a sign of failure, or that the counsellor could not help with their particular concern.

At Exeter University I started a Study Counselling service. It was soon used by about 5 per cent of first-year students and about half that proportion from later years. These figures suggest that while there are no massive problems about what is expected from students, they should not feel there is something wrong with them when they have difficulties. We all have learning difficulties sometimes.

Many student unions provide a Niteline service. Students seeking help, or simply wanting to talk to someone, can phone at any time of night when other services are not available. Some colleges allocate a second- or third-year student to act as guide and friend to first-years. Unlike relationships with tutors, these friendships can be allowed to wither naturally; but I have known some of them last a lifetime.

In many institutions the students' heads of department or the departmental secretaries are sources of informal help. Yet every college will say the same thing: 'If you want help, don't hesitate to ask.' The difficulty for them is not in helping, but in knowing when their help is needed.

Conclusion

It is not the purpose of this chapter to present a 'how to study guide'. There is a plethora of books for students on that subject. Rather, it attempts to show parents and others how demands placed upon students from their early childhood can influence their later behaviour. In that way it aims to promote under-standing. It concentrates on what students have to do – organise their time, read a great deal, learn from lectures and discussions, relate to other people and get help when needed.

The popular view of student life is that it is a time of freedom without responsibility. That is misleading. For most students it is undoubtedly enjoyable, but there are also financial, social and work pressures of a kind not faced by most adults.

Further reading
Ference Marton, Dai Hounsell and Noel Entwistle (eds), *The Experience of Learning* (Scottish Academic Press, 1984).

Chapter 8

ASSESSMENT OF STUDENTS

There's a fundamental problem when assessing students

All student assessment involves sampling their behaviour. But how can we know that the sample is typical? How can we know that the behaviour assessed gives a valid indication of how they will behave doing other things and in other circumstances? This problem bedevils all assessment. Consider two statements:

> People who are good at doing A are generally good at doing B.

> People who are good at doing A are not necessarily good at doing B.

I am happy to believe both these statements, yet they pull in opposite directions.

To believe that assessments in higher education are valid assumes that the first statement is true. It will be true insofar as A and B are similar. It's a matter of degree. Writing four essays in three hours is probably more like journalism than marketing, though all three activities involve the arts of communication and persuasion.

If you use the results of assessments, you assume the behaviour assessed is typical for your purpose. If it is not, the assessment is not valid for that purpose. But different people will use assessments for different purposes. So how could assessments in higher education be valid for all of them?

The important point is to recognise that people try to use examinations and other assessments for purposes for which they were not intended. Like any other instrument, assessments are best when they are purpose-designed. Those purposes can be classified into six broad groups.

What is assessment for?

To assess achievement

For this purpose, the examiner asks the question 'What can the student do?' and compares the answer with the course objectives. Ideally the course objectives will be stated in terms of what the students should be able to do. In practice, that is not possible. Course objectives are rarely very explicit. How can they be? Particularly in non-vocational subjects like history, English and physics, there cannot be a list of skills that each participant must achieve. Each student may legitimately achieve different things. Consider, for example, the aims of higher education given in Chapter 2. For this reason, most tests of achievement in higher education try to *survey* a wide range of knowledge and skills – or at least give students an opportunity to display them.

To predict future behaviour

Although examinations test students on a few selected topics at one particular point in time, they are often used to predict future performance on activities that are quite different. There is little evidence that their predictions are very accurate. For example many examinations consist of writing three or four essays in three hours. Most jobs do not. So why should employers think that being good at examinations now, will predict how well a student will do something quite different several years later? Of course many employers don't think that.

There are two points here. One is that people change. They learn. So how do you know that in the future they will behave as they did in the past? The other is the point with which we began. How far does competence at one thing predict competence at another?

To monitor progress

By comparing achievement at different stages of a course, intermittent assessments can be used to monitor students' progress.

To motivate

Intermittent assessments and examinations are powerful
motivators. In fact they can be too powerful and create anxiety.
Their patterns of anxiety are different. Just before Easter and
during the summer term, scarcely a seat can be found in most
college libraries as students revise for end of year examinations. For some students, the stress is greater than one
might wish so that counselling and student health services
are well used during this period. A good tip to deal with
examination anxiety is a homoeopathic remedy: take some
homoeopathic Gelsemium a couple of hours before the examination. It is not addictive and has no side effects.

Intermittent assessment is popularly called 'continuous
assessment', but it isn't continuous. On the contrary, it creates
periodic peaks of anxiety, particularly among mature students.
For mature students, there is often more at stake. Perhaps
they feel higher education is an opportunity that won't come
again. Perhaps they sacrificed their job, they are the only wage
earner and they feel guilty because they don't spend as much
time with their families as they would like. Having an understanding and supportive family is important for all students.
That is why students whose parents have experienced higher
education often experience less anxiety than 'first generation'
students.

To test teaching

It is sometimes assumed that if the examination results are
bad, the teaching cannot be much good. That may be so, but
the more examination results are said to reflect the performance of the teacher, the less likely they are to reflect the
potential of the students. So which do you want to assume?

At the level of school work there are often many teachers
teaching pupils taking the same GCSEs or O grades. So it is
possible to compare the performance of one teacher's pupils
with those of another. But in higher education, except where
several colleges take the same exams, most teachers set their
own assessments. So, even though the external examiner from
another institution can make comments, judging teachers
against a common standard is not possible.

To license to practise

In some subjects, the possession of certificates or degrees is a qualification that entitles the holder to practise in a particular profession. For example the government has recently allowed science graduates to teach in schools without a teacher training. However professional bodies usually inspect and accredit courses to maintain standards, not to lower them. For instance, the Engineering Institutions have imposed increasingly strict requirements upon the syllabus content for degree courses in engineering. Even so, accreditation cannot guarantee that every graduate will know everything an Engineering Institution might regard as essential. Examinations cannot ask questions on everything, and even if they did, a choice of questions allows students to avoid those subjects on which they feel the weakest.

There are problems of validity

Difficulties in test design

An assessment is valid only if it tests the abilities it is intended to test. But it only takes a few moments' thought to realise that it is extremely difficult to design an assessment that will test the aims of higher education. For example, a test of critical thinking should be different from a test of knowledge. Both tests should be different from tests of initiative, creative thinking, responsibility, interpersonal skills, vocational skills, scientific attitudes, hard work, and solving a host of different kinds of problems. This list of skills could be much longer. It might be possible to devise an examination that will test some of them, and test some of them more than others. But, if so, how do you get the right balance between them and how do you decide what the right balance is anyway?

How to train examiners

Let us suppose that the Board of Examiners overcomes all these difficulties when devising an assessment. How will the Board ensure that each examiner can recognise, say, problem-solving skills and distinguish them from critical thinking?

The marking system

How will examiners allocate marks for each of these skills? Whatever they decide, the marking system will break down because one candidate will do nothing but display knowledge, another will show great originality without much knowledge, a third may analyse all the possible answers to a question with commendable logic without showing much knowledge or originality, while a fourth may display mature and balanced judgement based more upon intuitive feelings and personal experience. The answers for each of these four candidates may have almost nothing in common. If you allocate 25 per cent of the marks for each of their qualities so that the value of the qualities adds up to 100 per cent, each candidate will fail. You could say that no one person could display all those qualities in the same answer and so it is all right to have the marks allocated for them adding up to well over 100 per cent. In effect, that is what most examiners do, but they don't do it in an additive way. A person who gives twice as many facts will not get twice the number of marks. Students are not judged on quantity, but on the quality of their work. What a student needs to do to move his mark from 90 per cent to 100 per cent is not more of the same thing that took him from 0 per cent to 10 per cent, but something totally different in quality.

Conclusion

In short, the validity of most examinations in higher education is open to question on three counts. First, it is difficult to design assessments that test high-level intellectual skills. The test setter has to work at an even higher level. Consequently the intellectual and other skills being judged are frequently not specified. Second, most examiners have no training in making these judgements. For example, research has shown that, although examiners talk about the importance of high levels of thinking, most give more marks for factual recall than they would care to admit. Finally there are no generally accepted examining techniques. For example, examiners will happily add marks together or calculate averages as if they were quantities. Examination marks are not numbers. They are qualities.

The unreliability of assessments

Most assessments in higher education are open to criticism as being unreliable. That is to say they give inconsistent results. Broadly speaking, there are three kinds of inconsistency.

Different examiners

There are inconsistencies between examiners. Some may be generous and some may be strict. Some may award a very narrow range of marks, while others will use the full range from 0 to 100. These inconsistencies can be corrected by simple statistical techniques. These inconsistencies do not matter very much provided examiners place candidates in roughly the same order. But, in general, they don't. They are more likely to do so if they are members of the same department or in some other way have a common background.

The external examiner system is supposed to correct this error. He or she is supposed to say whether standards are consistent with those in other institutions. But there is reason to think that the system does not work very well. Sometimes external examiners are chosen because they are known to a member of the department so that they, too, come from the same background. Being one visitor among many members of the department, the examiner often feels under strong group pressure not to criticise too many things.

Inconsistency of a single examiner

There is not only inconsistency between different examiners. Research suggests that the same examiner may give very different marks to the same piece of work on different occasions when the mark given the first time is not remembered.

Test reliability

Judging from other walks of life, there is also reason to think that some tests give more consistent results than others. The same thing has been found for tests given to schoolchildren, but 'test reliability' has not been so well researched at the higher education level.

Are standards comparable in different institutions and years?

A more serious problem is the comparability of examinations that purport to assess the same thing. The same subjects may be taught in 40 universities and 20 polytechnics, each apparently awarding the same degree, while the curricula and the standards of the examiners may have little in common. Once again we rely upon the external examiner, but even he or she is unlikely to have experience of more than three institutions in any given year. The idea that the examiner can carry a standard around in his or her head from one institution to another with unfailing accuracy from year to year is an implicit assumption of the examination system which is frankly ludicrous.

A similar problem applies to maintaining consistent standards from year to year in the same institution in the same subject. A related problem is that even in the same year, few students actually take the same examination when there is a choice of questions. They answer different combinations of questions which are necessarily different with different knowledge and different intellectual skills required. Yet the similarity of the examinations taken is commonly assumed.

Conclusion

The whole examination system at all levels makes massive assumptions about the mental skills required by examinees and the competence of examiners to judge them. There is remarkably little research into the mental processes of either.

Some factors related to examination performance

Exam technique

Table 8.1 shows relationship between certain characteristics of students and their performance in degree examinations. The higher the figure, the closer the relationship. There have been many studies of this kind and the results vary a great deal with the students' subjects. None the less most of the studies, like this one, show that by far the strongest relationship to performance in degree examinations is performance in first-year examinations. One explanation of this is that there are particular examination techniques which help a student to do

133

well but which are not very strongly related to anything else. In fact, other research has shown that some students learn the tricks of the trade on how to pass examinations and they use the tricks to good effect. Others know the tricks exist but don't bother to apply them; while a third group who perform least well, don't even realise that these strategies and tactics exist.

Table 8.1 Correlations with degree results of university students

	Correlation coefficient
First year university exam marks	0.57
A-level score	0.32
Self-rating of hardworking	0.29[1]
Motivation	0.19[1]
Hours studying	0.19[1]
Study methods	0.18[1]
Exam technique	0.17
Verbal aptitude	0.11
Introversion	0.11
Lack of distractions	0.10
Numerical aptitude	0.07
Emotional stability	0.03

Note: 1. These items are related to motivation to study.
Source: N. J. Entwistle, J. Nisbet, D. Entwistle and M. D. Cowell, 'The academic performance of students I: prediction from scales of motivation and study methods', *British Journal of Educational Psychology*, Vol. 41, part 3 (November 1971).

Adjustment to college environments

All this suggests that examination performance is dependent upon a collection of specific skills which are not generalisable to job skills or, indeed, the skills required in doing research. 'He is good at doing examinations so he must be good at doing other things' is, on this evidence, a false assumption. You will notice that the correlation between A-level results and degree performance three years later is much less than the correlation with first-year examinations in the same institution. This difference can partly be explained by the time gap being three years rather than two. But it seems likely that there is also an environmental factor. Some students adjust to college life better than others.

Study habits

These environmental factors may well be related to study habits. Those factors in Table 8.1 marked[1] are all related to students' motivation to study. It is known that the amount of study time and its regularity are related to degree performance. So are study skills and the conditions in which students work. For example, in one piece of research it was shown that students who were resident in a tower block at the University of Essex found it uncongenial for private study. They therefore spent less time on their work and performed less well in examinations. As we have seen in Chapter 7, how long students spend in private study depends upon their style of life and their pattern of friendships.

Family background

A student's family background is also related to examination performance. In particular, the support of the family is important. If the parents obtained higher education, they pass on helpful attitudes and advice; and the student is less likely to feel that he is out of his social group and has taken a three- or four-year journey into the unknown.

Social pressures

Social and emotional factors are among the most powerful influences upon a student's academic performance. For example when the parents' marriage has been held together by the presence of the child at home, when he or she goes to college, the strains begin to show. Sooner or later the student senses that all is not well and feels a pressure to go home frequently rather than concentrate upon academic work at college.

For most students it is very important to feel that they belong to a group. That group will influence their life-style, in particular their working style. Boy–girl relationships can be very intense at the age when most students go to college. Most people understand that. What they don't realise is that college life intensifies these pressures. For example, in most other walks of life boy–girl relationships can be very private. In halls of residence they can be very public. Furthermore residential life allows relationships to develop intensely and subside with great rapidity. These things disturb concentration and concentration is essential when studying.

Career certainty

Conversely, students who have chosen a career and are working to achieve it, feel more settled. They work with a purpose and perform slightly better than those whose careers are undecided. Not that students should be put under pressure to decide their careers. It is the pressure and anxiety that is harmful.

Academic contacts

Students also do better if they have more contact with academic staff and fewer complaints about the quality of teaching. I don't mean to imply cause and effect. The direction of cause and effect could be the other way round: students who perform badly in examinations may be more reluctant to contact teachers and may wish to justify their poor performance by blaming them.

Personality and social class

The factors considered so far are related to the student personality and social class. Students who are more anxious and introverted like Kim are more likely to study hard for long hours than students like Robin who are over-confident and sociable. Similarly, students' fathers who have occupations classified in social classes I and II are more likely to have received higher education.

An important personality factor is related to the students' attitude to authority. It is to do with authoritarian attitudes, dogmatism, fear of uncertainty and ambiguity, and a desire for things to be organised and structured. The effects vary with the student's subject. Students with authoritarian attitudes do better in engineering and the physical sciences (and law), while, in higher education, students with those attitudes will find the arts and social sciences more difficult.

Not intelligence

Finally, you will see from Table 8.1 that once students are selected for higher education, differences in verbal and numerical abilities are not strongly related to degree perform-ance. Of course a certain level of intelligence is necessary to survive as a student, but differences among students are not very great.

The need to diversify assessment methods

Human beings are capable of doing a very wide variety of things that could be judged by other people. Yet in academic examinations, there is an extraordinary concentration upon three-hour examinations requiring candidates to write three or four essays. There is a great need for research into how assessment systems could be diversified. Let us look at some of the factors that could be varied.

Terminal or intermittent assessment?

Typically essay examinations occur at the end of the course. These contrast with intermittent assessments which occur periodically throughout the course.

Fixed length or open-ended assessments?

Essay examinations are usually three hours long or some other fixed length of time. Course work, projects, dissertations and theses are open ended. They are therefore less intensive. It's a bit like the difference between the 400 metres and seeing how far you can run in a given period of time. Intermittent assessments with their periodic hurdles are more like the steeplechase. Different people are best suited to different events and the training required is quite different for each.

Measure the time taken to do a task

Within the period specified for most assessments in higher education, the tasks themselves are untimed. The examiner doesn't know, and probably doesn't care, whether a candidate took half an hour or an hour and a half to answer a given question. This is unlike a secretary taking a shorthand test where both the quality of what she does, and how long she

137

takes to do it, are factors assessed. The neglect of 'time taken' in higher education is curious because, in most aspects of human performance, it is a very sensitive measure. For example, two candidates could solve a mathematical problem but one might see the way to do it straight away while another might hesitate a long time. The proliferation of computer terminals makes information on how long a candidate takes to answer a question much more readily available to examiners than in the past. But, so far as I know, no one has experimented with this factor.

Maximum power or minimum standard?

Most academic examinations are 'maximum power' assessments while professional entrance examinations require a 'minimum standard' to be reached.

Pass–fail or grades?

Minimum standard assessments are usually of a pass–fail type while a range of grades are more commonly awarded in tests of maximum power.

A third option which is becoming increasingly popular is for the examiner to write descriptive profiles of each candidate's performance. These are called 'assessment profiles'. They are not only most useful to employers, but they give constructive feedback to candidates. In some cases, this permits them to work at their weak points. The desire to rank people in order of merit is a conceptual mistake. Different people have different qualities and should be valued for what they are. Jones may be better than Smith at one task, while on another, their merit is the other way round. It would be unfair to say that one of them is a better person than the other. It depends what you are talking about. The temptation to put people along a single line should be resisted.

Impressionistic, analytical or objective marking?

There are three different ways of judging examination performance. In 'impression marking' the examiner gives a number or a letter grade according to his subjective impression of the student's work. In 'analytical marking' a certain number of marks may be awarded for each item on a checklist of criteria. How far a candidate has satisfied a criterion can still be a little subjective. In objective tests (such as the multiple choice 'tick in a box' type used in some medical schools), the marking and grading is sufficiently objective that it can be done by computer.

The type of skills assessed

Examinations vary not only in their subject matter but in whether the skills tested are cognitive (to do with knowledge and thinking), affective (to do with attitudes, motivation and feelings) or motor (including manual and other physical skills). Owing to the historical dominance of university examinations over the whole educational system, educational assessments have concentrated almost entirely upon cognitive skills. Other aspects of human beings have been grossly neglected. Hopefully, the growth of profile assessments will enable examiners to value the variety of qualities different students have. In particular the introduction of profile assessments could place more value upon attitudes, personality and motor skills.

All tasks compulsory or offer a choice?

Because all assessments are a sampling process, examinations are highly selective in what they assess. They are made even more selective when candidates are offered a choice of questions. Understandably, candidates prefer to have a choice, but examinations are less valid and reliable when they do.

Implications

The skills taught and tested are too narrow

We've seen earlier that traditional examinations require a restricted range of skills. The skills required to write three or four essays in three hours in geography are much the same as those required to do the same thing when the subject is history, English, or sociology. That's why students who do well in one examination tend to be the students who do well in others, but they don't necessarily do so well when the skills required are something different. That's why I said the skills required in higher education ought to be more wide-ranging. We need to widen the skills we teach. That process has begun with an increase in the number of courses that include vocational experience.

Broaden the criteria for selecting students

Most students who reach higher education have already acquired many of the skills required for writing three-hour examinations. My worry is that the system eliminates a lot of people who are not good examinees, who not only merit higher education, but who could contribute much more to us all if they had it. We don't know the size of the problem. We do know there are a lot of people who drop out of the education rat race who later return and do quite well.

Play the examination game to win

Until the skills required are broadened, the best way to get a start in life is to concentrate on the narrow range of skills required at present. In short, it pays to play the system.

The best way to learn examination skills is to practise doing exams. It's a very obvious point, but it is very rare for students to sit down and work with that level of intensity for three hours. Imagine training an athlete to compete in the 1,500 metres. Surely you would get him to run 1,500 metres at some stage if not quite frequently – not so in education, perhaps because we half recognise that doing examinations is not what we really want our students to be able to do. We don't really believe in the system we are operating. It's just that we cannot think of a feasible alternative. That's precisely what I think we have got to do, and there are new technologies now that should make alternatives more feasible.

Conclusion

If you have read this chapter and you have a social conscience, you should feel a little uneasy about how we decide who are the 'best' students, and how others are rejected. Perhaps our assessment systems should search for that which is good in every man and woman – an open-minded search, not a predetermined test with fixed criteria. After all, an open-minded search is very consistent with the values of higher education.

Further reading

John Heywood, *Assessment in Higher Education* (Wiley, 1987).

Chapter 9

PROJECTS AND RESEARCH

Research is a process of seeking the truth. At the end of Chapter 3 I said, 'the search for, and the proclamation of, the truth as one sees it are the fundamental activities of higher education'. . . . 'To seek the truth is fundamental to freedom. To apply it is fundamental to progress.' So research should be a process common to all higher education, indeed all education in a free society. We should all be researchers now.

We should all be researchers now

Hitherto, in school education, and too often in higher education, there has been an emphasis upon the teacher presenting knowledge for pupils and students to remember and regurgitate on the examination paper, but there are signs that this is changing. The General Certificate of Secondary Education (GCSE) in England and Wales, combined with increasing vocational activities in school education throughout Britain, is increasing the amount of project work carried out by pupils in schools.

Under the government's Enterprise in Higher Education scheme (EHE), the Training Agency has offered institutions up to a million pounds over five years if all their students obtain work experience as part of their courses, and employers are involved in their assessment. In practice this means that the students will carry out projects. Many employers have a small project, piece of research or enquiry that never gets done because no one ever has the time. But, except during the holidays, 'come and go' student workers are more disruptive than helpful. (Incidentally, the scheme arose from the common belief that most students have no work experience. That's not true; not a lot, maybe; but educationally a little experience is very different from none. Even if we ignore all part-time students, those on sandwich courses and all continuing education students, and confine our attention only to full-timers, nearly half have been employed before they enter higher education and, in the government's loan survey, 59 per cent obtained vacation employment for an average of eight weeks per year – more than EHE can offer over three or four years.)

These developments are bound to affect higher education. Instead of recruiting students who have successfully passed A-level examinations, there will be an increasing number of students who have undertaken projects, either at school or at work, using techniques similar to those employed in research. Undergraduate courses will no longer be a proving ground from which students will then go on to do research at post-graduate level. There will be more of a research attitude among undergraduates. This is all for the good. The major adjustment required will be by the academic staffs in higher education, not by their students.

If parents and employers have never done any research, and most will not, they may have the same non-comprehension about what goes on in higher education as parents have had in the past 25 years about what goes on in primary schools. This chapter gives an understanding of some of the skills, frustrations and procedures involved.

Of course, the procedures for carrying out projects and research will vary enormously from one subject to another. I can only make sweeping generalisations here.

Twelve typical stages in research

1 Deciding the general area

Typically, the procedures will follow twelve stages. First of all, in the humanities the student will need to decide the general area he would like to research. Straight away, there is here a difference from undergraduate studies. The student negotiates the topic with his likely tutor. The teacher is not setting a topic that the student must study. Very likely the student will choose a tutor to suit his interests. Under CNAA regulations a postgraduate should have two supervisors. At PhD level (Doctor of Philosophy) at least one should have supervised to that level before.

At this stage, the student's ideas about what he wants to investigate may be very vague and broad. In science and engineering it is much more common for a possible supervisor to recommend specific topics, problems or areas for investigation in the light of industrial needs or research in progress in his department.

In the case of aspiring postgraduate research students, at this stage the potential supervisor is also probably weighing up whether to accept the student. The teacher has to decide whether the candidate is appropriately qualified, whether the necessary resources (such as library, computing, laboratory facilities and technical assistance) will be available, whether if from overseas the student's English is good enough, whether he thinks the student will complete the research in a reasonable amount of time and whether the supervision of this student doing this piece of research is in his list of priorities.

Once he has been taken on, the student and supervisor should discuss how they will work together and how often they should meet. The student has the responsibility to raise any difficulties however small, to say what kind of advice he finds most helpful and to give an annual report on his progress for the head of department. The supervisor has the responsibility to set standards, to maintain regular contact, to monitor progress, to provide opportunities for instruction in research methods, and at postgraduate level to arrange seminars to which the student will make a contribution.

2 An inventory of resources

At the second stage, the tutor is likely to send the student away to find out what the available resources are for investigating topics in his broad area of interest. In the past, students have often confined this search to the library. I suspect that with growing practical and occupational experience, combined with computers and other sources of information, the student of the future will have many more resources from which to choose.

If the student is writing a thesis, the college library will probably have copies of theses done by previous students. It is a good idea for students to look at some of these at this early

144

stage. It helps to set standards and to give some idea of what to aim for. To leave this until later sometimes results in narrowing the student's vision of what might be done and how it might be presented.

Throughout all the stages of doing a project, it is advisable for students to keep a rough notebook in which they jot down any ideas, however half-formed or foolish they may seem. This notebook is purely personal. It is quite a good idea to date each jotting so that the student can monitor the development of his own ideas. It can be quite encouraging for students to realise how they have progressed. It is also quite a good idea to initial those ideas that are the student's own. It is also vital to keep a record of all bibliographic sources that have been consulted. Trying to find out the detail of references previously consulted can be extremely time-consuming later on.

3 Narrowing the field

Whether or not there is an abundance of resources, the tutor will encourage the student to narrow down the area of interest to something minute and manageable. Students always choose topics that are too big because they do not realise how much there is to know. The sooner a student can narrow down his topic of investigation, the less time is needed to study topics that will later be discarded as irrelevant to the investigation.

4 Specifying the precise research problem

The fourth stage is to decide the theme or problem that the student wants to justify, criticise or solve. There are four characteristics of a good problem. It must be clearly, simply and precisely stated. It must be limited in scope. It should be consistent with most, but not necessarily all, known facts. And it should be verifiable both in principle and in practice. The practical limitations include the time required for the project, the student's budget, his/her ability and ensuring the necessary co-operation of other people, such as the general public in a social survey or lab technicians in chemistry. A very important fifth characteristic is required for postgraduate research degrees, particularly PhDs – a degree is only awarded for original work, so the problem must allow originality.

In practice, the theme or problem nearly always has to be progressively refined and modified to make it more precise and consistent with the known facts. Its progressive refinement continues to take place during the next four stages.

Specifying the problem is a crucial stage in any research. The research cannot begin until it is clear. Furthermore the CNAA will not accept a student's registration for a research degree until it is clear what the student wants to investigate. Most university faculty boards are the same.

5 Getting the topic and oneself organised

The fifth stage is to plan the organisation of the project. The student needs to plan his time and to outline the possible argument that his project or thesis will present. Of course this is only tentative at this stage but the steps of an argument each have to be justified and so those steps show what has to be investigated to make each justification possible.

A wise student will make sure that he lets his supervisor see his organisation at this stage. The organisation is crucial to showing how the argument or thesis is developed. A supervisor and his/her student should arrange to meet once a week to discuss progress.

6 Labelling rough notes

Having decided how the eventual presentation is likely to be organised, the sixth stage is to mark these notes and jottings with a number or some other indication of where the ideas might be used. Very many may not be used at all and can be discarded.

7 Planning observation

Another consequence of deciding the organisation and likely plan of the project is that the student can decide much more easily what is relevant and what is irrelevant by reading and studying selectively.

While reading selectively, the student will continue to jot down ideas and thoughts in a rough notebook. In particular, he/she will consider what fieldwork, experiments or other investigations need to be carried out to justify the theme or to solve any problem. This stage includes designing experiments, questionnaires and other instruments for observations. It includes working out what could be inferred from all possible observations in advance of making them. This avoids going to a lot of trouble to conduct experiments or make other observations and then discovering that they could not possibly prove anything anyway. These activities need to be prepared and their detail incorporated into the plan outlined at stage 5.

8 Observation

The eighth stage is to carry out that fieldwork, laboratory work or other form of investigation. Again, it is necessary to jot down observations at the time because they will not be remembered later. This is particularly important where the student has to report on methods and procedures. Many thoughts and observations occur during practical work which cannot be recalled later. So these too need to be captured at the time and recorded in the student's notebook. Quite often, these thoughts lead the student to modify his/her argument, diagnosis of the problem or suggested solution to it. Indeed, this is the purpose of a pilot investigation. Consequently, it is not unusual for the student to return to stage 4 and to go through to stage 8 again. In some forms of postgraduate research, this cycle is repeated many times. For example, in literary research, a student may revise his/her opinion and argument.

9 Planning the presentation of work done

Stage 9 is to plan the presentation of the project. Of course this will vary enormously with the subject. In art and architecture, it may consist of a display with almost no written material at all. In computing, it might consist of programmes or files on a floppy disk. In some other subjects, it may consist of little more than the results of a calculation. What I shall present here is typical of the requirements for many of the social sciences. What is required in arts subjects on the one hand, and the physical sciences on the other is different in degree rather than of a totally different kind.

First, the student needs to set his/her problem or theme in

its context. The student needs to present a review of the literature as part of this context, not as a separate exercise presented before the real issues are considered. The bibliography
will need to be built up as references are made. The context
will include the background of the subject, an explanation of
why this project was undertaken and not another one, its
theoretical and/or its practical implications, and possible hypotheses, themes or arguments that could be explored.

Next, the aim of the project needs to be set out in a way
that is precise, objective, non-emotive, non-judgemental, and
factual. The student should use concise, short and reasoned
sentences.

When describing the method of investigation, the acid test
is 'Could the investigation be replicated from this description?'
So quite a bit of detail needs to be included in this section and
some of it (e.g. sample questionnaires) may be included in an
appendix. It should always be remembered that constructive
criticism is the fundamental process of higher education. So
the student needs to justify what he has done and anticipate
objections. In particular, there is a need to explain the use
of experimental methods, questionnaires, interviews, direct
observations, participative research, or any other method.
There is also a need to explain the design of the investigation.
For example, if one thing is being compared with another,
what controls are observed to ensure that the comparison is a
fair one? The student needs to explain and justify the criteria
and/or the measuring instruments used. For example, can they
be justified as convenient or because they have previously been
used by other researchers? The student also needs to consider
whether other criteria are relevant or possible.

Most projects and investigations involve sampling. In many
projects, there is a need to justify the size of the sample,
whether it is typical and how it is obtained.

The principle of replication requires that the student's procedure should be succinctly explained in a matter of fact style.
Where equipment has been used (e.g. in the physical sciences)
it should be described. Where instructions or questions have
been devised (e.g. in the social sciences) these should be specified.

Almost no matter what the project, the student gathers a mass of information and data. The problem is how to present these findings or results clearly. What information can be put in diagrams? What can be tabulated? Very often the presentation of results reveals that certain unexplored and unexpected relationships should be investigated. These further investigations should be restricted to those that are relevant and, in practice, are often restricted by the time available. Yet it is remarkable how often students present sets of data without ever considering how they might be related. Another very common error in the presentation of results is to give an interpretation of them. It is important to stick to the facts objectively at this stage and to distinguish data from their interpretation. Interpretation is presented after the results and is always more subjective and controversial.

The interpretation of data and their relationships are commonly considered in a 'Discussion' section. Part of a student's critical skill lies in the questions he asks himself. How are the data related to research reviewed at the beginning? How do they fit existing theories and, most of all, how can they be applied to the student's problem, hypothesis, or argument? What are the limitations of the data? What factors influenced the results and what reservations does the student have when making any interpretation? What objections might other people make to these interpretations? What points might be conceded to the student's opponents and how will rejected criticisms be rebutted?

The conclusion should summarise the findings of the project in terms of the aims presented at the beginning and giving the crucial evidence that supports or defeats those aims.

Finally, the student should write an abstract which summarises the structure and sequence of the project. This abstract will be placed at the beginning, after the title page but before the contents page.

10 Preparing the physical appearance of the presentation
Many examining authorities have quite strict regulations about how theses and other projects should be presented. For example they may say that there should be three copies typed

with double spacing on a certain size of paper bound in a certain way with gold lettering of a specific size on the outside and a specified form of words on the title page inside. Ideally students should look at these regulations at stages 2 or 5. Stage 10 is the very latest.

The thing to avoid is to start writing up or preparing illustrations without having a clear conception of the physical appearance of the work. Similarly it is important to prepare illustrations, maps, tables, photographs or any other visual material before writing up. Not only can a picture save a thousand words, but if the illustrations are not done first, they tend not to illustrate the text because the text is not written with reference to them.

It is a common error to start writing up too soon. It feels good to get a chapter or two out of the way early, but it usually results in the argument not hanging together, because the student has started to write before it can be seen how all the facts interconnect. To write rough notes early is a good idea; to attempt the final version early is folly. This error is all the more tempting now that wordprocessors give the illusion that modifications can easily be made later. Details can; but it is very difficult to change the whole tone of an argument, once one's mind has committed itself to seeing the subject in one (less mature) way.

11 Writing up

Several points need to be made about the style of the write-up itself. First, it should be consistent. So there should be a consistent hierarchy, numbering and style of headings. The same applies to tables, graphs and other illustrations, as well as to footnotes and appendices. There are two or three accepted ways of setting out bibliographical references. Whatever style is chosen, the student should be consistent.

As I have suggested, the language should be crisp and simple, but that is not always easy because, by their nature, the topics are often quite complex. For this reason, the student has to teach the technical terms of this subject to his reader as he goes along. The same applies to abbreviations and acronyms.

Another major difficulty is what to include and what to leave out. It is usually best to leave out jokes, anecdotes and personal whims. It is also usually best to include some self-criticisms and reservations about one's conclusions. What is not so clear is whether to include abortions and digressions. By 'abortions', I mean those parts of the project the student undertook which came to nothing. Many projects and research involve exploring avenues which turn out to be cul-de-sacs. They turn out to be a waste of time, yet the student may have learnt something from them which influences the eventual outcome of the project. In this case, it seems right to include something about the exploration that was abandoned. Influential abortions have to be mentioned. The same applies to digressions. The student should exclude irrelevant digressions but include those that are necessary as briefly as possible.

Above all, the student should remember that he/she is writing an argument. The truth is being sought by a process of criticism and now the task is to seek to persuade the readers of what has been found. The steps of the argument can be made clearer by the use of quintessential headings which, read in sequence, summarise the argument. Another trick is to imagine that what is written is always being contested by a hostile critic. By anticipating and answering all the objections to the argument, the thesis will be made all the stronger. Another tip to make the argument clearer is to provide 'tracking devices'. That is to say, other parts of the project should be referred to so that the leader can follow the argument as a whole. The most important 'tracking device' is the abstract or summary that should appear at the beginning. This should be written last so that it reflects the structure and sequence of the project as a whole.

12 Take a holiday, review, amend and present

When the first full draft of a thesis or project is complete parents and friends may need to persuade the student to take a break from it. Every author knows the problem of being so close and bound up in one's subject that one cannot see it from the point of view of the reader. That's the time to take a holiday. The student will see what has been written in a different light, and see it as a whole, on returning after a fortnight. That is the time to make amendments. Even the abstract can be written then. After that, with the supervisor's consent, it can go to the binders and then to assessment.

At this time the student often experiences contradictory feelings. Parents and friends may need to appreciate them. On the one hand there is great relief that it is finished; on the other, anxiety and tension about a viva examination or what the assessor will think of it.

The lonely life of the postgraduate research student

The previous section gave a general account of what a student has to do regardless of whether he/she is doing an under-graduate project or postgraduate research. But postgraduate research is bigger in scope, takes longer, is more thorough, demands originality and often results in a different lifestyle.

It is the difference in life-style that sometimes takes a student by surprise and leaves parents at home not understanding what has changed. Imagine a student who goes away to university, enjoys the time spent there, gets on very well in the department, does well in final exams and is asked to stay on to do research. When the student begins research his/her friends have left. There is no longer a regular diet of lectures and seminars. The tutor is seen briefly only once a week. The social life of the university is beginning to get repetitive. The student feels unsure in unexplored academic territory.

All this adds up to being lonely. Parents at home realise that the student's attitude has changed, but they are in no position to know what is different. Don't get me wrong: most postgraduates thoroughly enjoy their work and often find the release from the drudge of lectures and exams a breath of fresh air. None the less the experience of loneliness has happened sufficiently often to warrant a mention.

The role of the supervisor is crucial. According to one study, most postgraduates prefer him/her to be knowledgeable, available for consultation, helpful, stimulating and critical in that order of importance. When asked about the difficulties they encountered students mentioned isolation, their inadequate knowledge of research methods and the need to limit the size of their project. Part-timers mentioned the lack of time.

You may wonder why some of the cleverest young people in the land wish to spend up to five of the best years of their lives investigating an apparently remote and esoteric problem. There are two kinds of answer. First they do it out of interest, personal advancement, self-fulfilment and because they enjoyed their first degree. Second, the problems are not usually remote and esoteric when their implications are understood.

Although there has often been a fuss about the number of PhD students who don't complete their degree successfully, 84 per cent are successful in science and engineering subjects (coincidentally the same figure as for undergraduates in those subjects). Only 70 per cent are successful in the humanities, but as very few of them are supported by taxpayers' money, the fuss is less justified.

Research students normally write a thesis, which they must discuss and defend against the criticisms of two or three examiners, the third of whom might be their own supervisor. This sounds pretty daunting, but most examiners are kindly without relaxing the standards they treasure.

The funding of academic research

Research is a major activity of higher education institutions, particularly universities. It is important to stress this now because the balance of this book may give the impression that teaching alone matters. In universities, teaching and research are regarded as equally important. Whatever the protestations of Vice-Chancellors, academic promotion is more on the basis of research than teaching. In the public sector too, research is highly rewarded even though, or perhaps because, little or no time is allocated for it. Roughly half the expenditure of universities is for teaching and half for research, 30 per cent on sponsored research projects and 20 per cent from the Universities Funding Council (UFC). That is from the taxpayer. The proportions spent on broad subject areas are similar to those of other major research countries (see Table 9.1).

Having said that, it must be admitted that little more than 10 per cent of research expenditure in Britain is allocated to higher education; 64 per cent is for defence. The Departments of Health, Social Security, Transport, Environment and Employment each spend a little money on research while the Departments of Trade and Industry, and Agriculture and Fisheries spend rather more. True, each of these departments subcontract some of their research to higher education institutions, but that only amounts to about 2 per cent of the whole.

Table 9.1 Percentage of government-funded expenditure on research in nine subject areas

	UK	International average[1]
Engineering	16	13
Physical sciences	22	21
Environmental sciences	7	5
Maths and computing	5	4
Life sciences (including medicine)	34	38
Social sciences[2]	6	6
Professional and vocational	5	5
Arts and humanities	6	7
Multi-discipline	1	0
Total	100	100

Notes:
1. The international average is the average percentage for UK, USA, France, Federal Republic of Germany, Japan and the Netherlands.
2. These figures include psychology.
Source: Advisory Board for the Research Councils, 1987.

The cutbacks in government spending in the 1980s have severely reduced British research. Although its reputation still lingers, Britain is no longer a major source of research. On one estimate 5 per cent of research is British. There used to be pride in the good proportion of Nobel prizes coming to Britain. The proportion is now no higher than for other European countries. France and Germany spend 50 per cent more on research than Britain. Research is an essential investment and the British economy will suffer even though the cutbacks were supposed to save it.

What are the functions of research? Why should money be spent on it? There are three main groups of functions.

First there are functions concerned with the development of

science, new ideas, scientific standards, the bases upon which
new fields of knowledge grow and can be quickly applied (e.g.
the application of transistors in the 1970s) and the interlink-
ing of academic disciplines. Money for these functions comes
from three main sources: the research councils in the form of
research contracts with specific institutions; local authorities
in the form of student grants; and the UFC as part of the 20
per cent mentioned above.

A second group of functions is concerned more with applied
research and development than with fundamental discoveries.
Their immediate effects are economic and social, rather than
a permanent contribution to a body of knowledge. The contracts are mostly with industry and government. They include
contributions to government enquiries, strategic research,
applications of new ideas to industry, and checking the feasi-
bility of plans, proposals and policies.

A third group consists of contributions to the educational
and cultural life of the nation. The money comes mostly from
local authorities in the form of student grants and from individuals in the form of their fees. These functions include
advancing knowledge, creating an enquiring attitude of mind
in the community, fostering national, community and individual awareness, and producing future generations of scientists,
teachers and other professions.

In the 1980s there has been a growing emphasis on the
second group. However, because this group depends upon the
first, in the long run that emphasis will be self-defeating if a
balance is not maintained.

It now seems likely that the 20 per cent from the UFC will
diminish or disappear and the money be given to the research
councils. There will be competition between institutions for
that money. Funds will be allocated selectively and 'unto them
that already hath, more shall be given'. The government
believes that selective funding will produce centres of excellent
research. Unfortunately the mix of people and circumstances
that result in high levels of creativity is not so predictable.

The allocation of funds will determine areas of new knowledge. It is the arts, humanities and social sciences that will
suffer most by diverting funds to the research councils. Table

9.2 shows there is no research council for the arts to redistribute the money that previously went to the UGC and the UFC. (The Arts Council supports the practice of music, the theatre and other arts. Its funds are already quite inadequate and it is not conceived as a council for research to which academics may submit proposals.) Furthermore the Economic and Social Research Council now receives only 3 per cent of the money allocated to the research councils. (More than ten times as much is spent on nuclear physics as on all the social sciences put together.) Yet, it is the social sciences that have developed most rapidly in the past 50 or 60 years. They are just as likely to contribute to economic prosperity as research in the sciences. They are also more likely to produce informed comment about government policies.

Table 9.2 Breakdown of Research Councils' expenditure by main area of activity

	Science budget (%)
Agriculture and Fisheries Research Council	
Administration	1.7
Plant sciences	1.4
Animal physiology and genetics	1.2
Food	1.1
Arable crops	1.1
Animal disease	0.7
Horticulture	0.5
Grassland and animal production	0.4
Postgraduate awards	0.2
Engineering	0.1
Total 8.3	
Economic and Social Research Council	
Economic and social research	2.1
Postgraduate awards	1.2
Administration	0.4
Total 3.7	

Table 9.2 *(continued)*

Medical Research Council

Cell biology and disorders	6.9
Physiological systems and disorders	3.7
Neuroscience and mental health	3.2
National Institute of Medical Research	1.9
Clinical Research Centre	1.7
Administration	1.4
Postgraduate awards	1.0
Tropical medicine	0.5

Total 20.6

Natural Environment Research Council

Earth sciences	2.5
Marine sciences	2.5
Terrestrial and freshwater sciences	2.2
Antarctic research	2.0
Postgraduate awards	1.0
Administration	0.7

Total 10.8

Science and Engineering Research Council

Nuclear physics	12.7
Engineering	9.8
Science	9.6
Postgraduate awards	8.6
Astronomy and planetary science	8.2
Central support	2.1
Administration	2.1

Total 53.1

Other sources

Total 3.8

Grand total 100.0

Source: Advisory Board for the Research Councils, 1987.

Conclusion

My conclusion is both optimistic and pessimistic. Changes in schools may make research skills more common. In higher education government controls may restrict knowledge and freedom. To that we must now turn.

Further reading

Advisory Board for the Research Councils, *A Strategy for Science Base* (HMSO, 1987).

Chapter 10

WHAT ACADEMIC FREEDOM IS: WHY IT MATTERS

Most members of the public understand the freedom of the press and they know why it is important. But they do not understand what academic freedom is, nor why it matters. It seems as if academics are claiming a freedom for themselves, a special privilege. Ordinary people resent others seeming to claim special privileges. The freedom of the press is seen as important for everyone. Academic freedom is not seen in the same way. But it ought to be. Both are about freedom of information – freedom to know the truth.

In one way academic freedom is even more precious. It is not a freedom for big business, for newspaper tycoons or television sponsors. It is a freedom for individuals from which everyone benefits. Yet it does involve claiming a special right and that claim needs to be justified. The arguments are not easy; so you may find they need a lot of thought.

There are two complementary arguments, one based upon a group of general civil liberties, the other upon the special nature of academic work. Both arguments are required to justify academic freedom as a special right.

The General and Special Arguments

The General Argument

According to the General Argument, any citizen in a democratic country is free (a) to seek the truth about anything he likes and (b) to pass it on to others, unless these two freedoms are explicitly taken away.

They are taken away in the case of military secrets, recent Cabinet papers, one company's chemical formulae, another company's production processes, certain aspects of personal privacy and so on. For most employees these freedoms are also surrendered during working hours, because it is implicit in their contracts that their time will be spent on the employer's business, not seeking and proclaiming the truth. But of course, in the special case of higher education, that *is* the employer's business. It is a lecturer's job to seek and proclaim the truth as he sees it, not as others see it. It would therefore be contrary to the implicit contract between employer and employee to take those two freedoms away, to sack, or penalise in some other way, a lecturer who exercised either of them.

The Special Argument

According to the Special Argument, academics claim a special authority and privilege not possessed by the general population as a civil right. The crux of the Special Argument is:

- a claim that academics have a special competence or expertise in the search for truth; and
- a claim that academics possess a special knowledge of their subject.

This distinction is important. Ultimately to deny the first claim is to suppress the truth. To deny the second is to challenge the intellectual authority of academics. None the less both claims overlap in that, if academics carry out research, they can claim knowledge not possessed by others, because they have explored and tested ideas at the frontiers of knowledge not visited by others.

Some assumptions

The General and the Special Arguments make a number of assumptions.

Functions

Both arguments depend upon the assumption that the functions of institutions of higher education include seeking and disseminating the truth within their specific areas of competence.

Choosing what to teach and research

If academics are free to disseminate the truth as they see it within their areas of competence, that should include the freedom to teach what they see as being true in those areas. That doesn't mean that any students should be forced to attend. It does mean that academics should not be forced to teach anything they think is not true. But they might be obliged to teach truths that they don't want to teach. We all have to do parts of our jobs that we don't like.

Similarly academics may be free to research any problem within their areas of competence (except those, like state secrets, which are explicitly debarred). But these arguments do not prevent them from being required to research topics not of their choice.

Contracts

They also assume there is an implicit contract between an academic and his/her institution that allows the academic certain freedoms. In particular, on the Special Argument, unlike most employees' contracts, the implied contract doesn't necessarily bind the academic to do exactly what the employer wants. The contract isn't, and cannot be, to prejudge, find and proclaim particular assertions to be true. It is to seek, find and proclaim the truth irrespective of what the institution might think about it. Thus an academic should not be penalised for finding and publishing unpopular truths.

Free critical enquiry

Both arguments make assumptions about how knowledge is obtained. As we saw in Chapter 3, since the time of Descartes, the accepted methods for obtaining knowledge have not been to refer to the dogma of presupposed authorities, but have included independent observation, the principle of public verification, the replication of experiment, and the dissemination, testing and contesting of opinions. This process of critical enquiry, in which no belief is immune from doubt, has become fundamental to the pursuit of knowledge in higher education.

Civil liberties

Whatever the exceptions, the General Argument assumes certain civil liberties as the norm in our society, in particular, the rights to discover and disseminate the truth unhindered.

The value of knowledge based upon its consequences

There could be two different assumptions about the value of academic freedom based upon its consequences. In our kind of society it is easier than in some others, to value knowing the truth, not only as sometimes useful, but as having some intrinsic and possibly absolute value. For example, academics such as F. R. Leavis claimed to study a subject 'for its own sake', not for its beneficial application or other consequences. In societies without our civil liberties, academic freedom would have to be given as a special privilege. It would probably, though not necessarily, be given because the knowledge resulting from such freedom was seen as useful or beneficial.

Why does academic freedom matter?

It is essential to the preservation of democracy. That is why I said at the beginning of this chapter that academic freedom is important for everyone, not just academics.

The first thing any undemocratic government does is to try to control the minds of its people. In a democracy, there is a sense in which, ultimately, the minds of the people control the government. Nowadays the first thing any revolution or counter-revolution tries to do is to control the radio and television stations. It is they, more than the newspapers, that have most immediate control over the information available to the people.

How can the people decide what is true, what is biased opinion, and what is propaganda? They need two things: the best possible methods and resources for finding out; and independent voices so that the findings are impartially interpreted and expressed.

Academics provide both these things when they have the freedom to do so. The best possible methods are research methods, and academics have the necessary expertise. Independence necessitates freedom from pressures and vested interests. Academics speak out with independent minds when they have the necessary freedom.

That is why their freedom is important. That is why academics and universities are often the first to suffer at the hands of repressive governments and why universities are often the first sources of protest.

We should be clear that it is not only governments that wish to control information or to present facts in a particular light. Commercial interests may wish to do the same. For example it was not in the interests of the tobacco industry to research the effects of smoking upon health. Their advertisements and sponsorships deliberately associated smoking with healthy activities like sport. Nor was it in the short-term interests of successive governments. Governments obtained substantial revenues from tobacco taxes.

It was university research that showed the effects and the broadcasting media that publicised them. History is now repeating itself with the effects of alcohol. Its harm has been known for centuries, but only by its harm being thoroughly demonstrated can the political power of the brewing lobby be defeated. As with smoking, millions will suffer and die until the truth is fully known. These are only two examples. The marketing and persuasion industries are now big business.

A higher education system dependent upon commerce and industry will not seek or proclaim the truth, because it will not be financed to find the truths that commerce and industry do not want to face, do not want others to know, and which they see as having no value to them. Fundamental research, which may at first sight appear to have no obvious application, will be neglected. Laser technology and microwave ovens would not exist if academics had not been funded to explore freely ideas that industry thought were useless.

During the 1980s it was government policy to increase the dependence of higher education upon commerce and industry. To that extent there has been a loss of freedom. The government itself has used its power to influence what information is available to the public. The BBC was so pressured not to show certain programmes that its Director General resigned. The author of *Spycatcher* was pursued vindictively in the international courts. Research funds have diminished and the number of university departments funded to do research is expected to be reduced. Not least in the field of education itself, research has virtually been restricted to topics related to the government's own policies. Then its publication has been restricted when the findings have not supported those policies (e.g. research into the 'popularity' of school boards and parent power).

In 1988 the government tried to prevent the following amendment to the Education Reform Act passing into law: the University 'Commissioners shall have regard to the need to ensure that academic staff have freedom within the law to question and test received wisdom, and to put forward new ideas and controversial or unpopular opinions, without placing themselves in jeopardy of losing their jobs or privileges they may have at their institutions'. The government failed. The reader should answer, 'Why did it try; and why did it fail?'

Against this, many previous governments have worked to preserve academic freedom and other democratic rights. Governments have supported the rights and practices of their oppositions because they recognise that the processes of democracy are not only of greater value than their own policies, but belong to a higher-order of values. The difference is like the difference between 'statesmanship' and 'political skill'.

Academic freedom to pursue and proclaim the truth as one sees it, is a higher order value of this kind. To say that where governments pay for research, governments should control what is researched and what is published, is to fail to understand this point. Industries may commission research for their exclusive use. Government sponsorship of research, unlike commercial and industrial sponsorship, should not be in its own interests, but on behalf of its people; and it has an obligation to let the people know its findings. That is a different kind of responsibility.

The crucial conclusion is that academics need to be financed by governments to seek and proclaim the truth wherever it leads them, because that should be part of governments' policies to preserve and enhance democracy. This requires that governments trust academics and that academics earn that trust. Both have obligations towards the other. There's nothing wrong in mutual trust; no family, or any other relationship, can survive without it. Mutual trust is strengthened when it is constantly tested and constantly passes the test. In this respect academic freedom is no different from any other freedom.

Further reading

Malcolm Tight (ed.), *Academic Freedom and Responsibility* (Society for Research into Higher Education, 1988).

Chapter 11

THE GOVERNMENT AND
FINANCE OF
INSTITUTIONS

The general character of academic management

Some people see universities, polytechnics and colleges as run
by a Prime Ministerial figure called a Vice-Chancellor, Director or Principal who is chosen by a 'sovereign' who is either
the Chancellor of a University as Chairman of the University
Court, or, in the case of the polytechnics and colleges, the
Chairman of the Governing Body. Other people think of universities as elite institutions governed by an elite of the elite,
namely a group of senior professors who discuss, persuade and
cajole over a glass of port in the senior common room after
lunch. Non-academic staff will see their institution as being
run by the academics. Junior academic staff may feel dominated by departmental pressures, particularly the whims of
their head of department. Heads of departments will see themselves as trying to accommodate all the wishes of individuals
in their department within institutional policies, financial constraints and student numbers laid down. Students may think
they are governed by an impersonal set of rules and unwritten
precedents followed by a group of equally faceless adminis-
trators who always seem to be acting at the behest of an
inscrutable committee. In the public sector higher education
(PSHE) there may be a feeling that the college or polytechnic
is run by a group of laymen on the governing body who have
little understanding or sympathy with the particular needs of
academic work.

Although each of these perceptions may have a small
element of truth, each impression is a travesty of academic
government. The way decisions are taken in academic govern-

ment is far more subtle and complex. No doubt this is why people talk about 'academic politics'.

The process is political in the sense that there is management and manipulation of power. Rules are made or changed and there are sanctions that can be applied to ensure that they are observed. These rules are the result of discussions in which conflicting interests and perspectives will be expressed. Furthermore, academic institutions have explicit policies which they try to pursue and which are distinct from the aims and objects of their individual members. Counterparts could be found for each of these features in national government, but so they could in a factory or almost any other organisation.

There are other respects in which academic politics are quite different from national politics. For one thing there are no political parties. Membership of an institution is more temporary than membership of a nation. This leads to a different pattern of membership and commitment that is more intense, but more short-lived. Academics choose their institution, while very few of us choose the nation to which we belong.

Furthermore, and this is important, in most academic institutions there is not a simple line management forming a hierarchy of power. Most lecturers have several interests and obligations – they may teach on several courses and be involved in more than one research project, each having a different leader. Lecturers largely manage their own time and prioritise their own work. Until recently this meant that there were no clear lines of accountability and academic management had to be more by incentives than sanctions. Indeed the procedures of line management encouraged in universities by the Jarratt Committee (1985) and in the public sector by the NAB Committee (1985) (see Chapter 3) are drawn from the world of industry and sit uncomfortably in an academic setting, particularly where research is a priority.

As Charles Handy of the London Business School has pointed out, academic institutions are managed by consent, not consensus. Management needs to check that what they propose is acceptable. Individuals want to be consulted rather than participate in management. Authority is not imposed from above, but by consent from below. Academics see them-

167

selves as a resource. They want the right to disagree based upon reciprocal respect and trust.

Academic institutions are not like industry. An academic is judged by his/her peers, not least by those in the same field in other institutions. That would be extraordinary in textile or motor manufacture. In a factory many people work together to produce relatively few products. Individuals on the assembly line may have little idea how their work contributes to the whole. The co-ordination is therefore an essential feature of management. In the academic world the same degree of co-ordination is not intrinsic to the methods of production. While individuals may work together to do research, to write a publication or to teach a course, research, teaching and publication can be very individual activities. Idiosyncratic individuals are to be encouraged. It may be their idiosyncrasies that challenge old ideas to produce new ones. While supporting work may be divided between several research assistants, the academic product, that is the formation of ideas, is necessarily the product of individual minds. Ideas are part of a person. Manufactured goods are not. Ideas are assembled in the mind. So the 'academic assembly worker' and 'the manager of ideas' have to be the same person. In this respect an academic is necessarily his or her own manager because of the nature of the product.

The intrinsic individualism of academic work means there is a constant organisational conflict between the needs of the individual, or very small units, and the management of the institution as a whole. This conflict produces a tension which is also creative, because there are always forces for change and hence adaptation. That may surprise those readers who think of universities as ancient unchanging institutions. They have a misconception. Universities have survived because they have adapted. They have been able to adapt because they are managed by a constantly shifting balance of forces, not rigid management structures. It is this shifting balance that is subtle and where academic politics lies.

Academic departments

In most universities, polytechnics and colleges, apart from individuals, the basic unit is the academic department. Departments are the units to which most lecturers feel they belong. True, they belong to faculties, schools or other larger units too; but lecturers label themselves and each other as chemists, mathematicians, historians etc. according to their disciplines, and departments tend to be collections of staff with a common discipline. Collectively they have an authority with reference to teaching and research in their subject. Consequently they have some autonomy and higher levels of management must defer to them. Consequently academic government has a consultative and federal character that is not typical of most areas of employment.

The balances of power are also complex within departments. Members of departments have different status according to their ranks (e.g. lecturer, senior lecturer, reader, professor) and different amounts of power according to their personalities, involvement, power of language and so on.

The head of department has the most power. He or she will speak for his/her colleagues at meetings of wider groups such as faculty boards and senate. Accordingly the head of department is likely to be at the centre of a wheel of communications, and will argue the departmental case at committees for resources such as finance and staffing. More than anyone the head takes decisions on behalf of the department and, having probably achieved his/her ambition in the university or polytechnic, the head is in a position to resist the demands of popularity when the need arises. The head will write references for students and will be very influential in departmental promotions and appointments. Particularly if the head is a professor, he or she is likely to serve professional and academic organisations outside the institution and thereby be a member of a wider network of contacts. These contacts and experiences give more information to the head and strengthen any personal influence in the department. However, in the last twenty years non-professorial heads of department, elected by their peers, have become common. Very often the appointment is

169

for a limited term, while in the past professorial appointments often included the duties of headship.

Faculties

Faculties and 'schools' are groups of kindred subject departments, such as the arts, the social sciences, the natural sciences, engineering and medicine. Most students, but by no means all, will take their main and subsidiary subjects from departments within a single faculty. To ensure common standards entry qualifications for students may be the same across a faculty. Some departments may be members of more than one faculty. For example geography and psychology may be members of the social and natural science faculties and they might require different entry qualifications for students taking science and social science degrees.

In a typical university such regulations are laid down by the senate on the recommendation of a faculty board presided over by a dean who is part-time. At one time the dean would almost always have been a senior professor, but non-professorial deans are increasingly common; and, deans being chosen from a wider pool of staff, standards have risen at just the time (with severe financial constraints, departmental closures, early retirements and new methods of staff appraisal) that fine qualities of management have been most needed.

Because, in higher education, the individual is a productive unit, a very large number of communication links are required between central management and each productive unit. That is a big problem often not appreciated by academics themselves. Faculty boards are intermediaries for communication. There being too many departments, central university committees are often composed of faculty representatives whose reports need to be relayed to individuals by departmental representatives on faculty boards.

Faculty boards also exercise quality controls on behalf of senates. They can provide a wider yet informed view of the work of their constituent departments. They vet proposals to do with courses, including their content, methods and examiners. In particular they watch the comparability of courses claiming comparable standards.

In PSHE the Council for National Academic Awards has, until recently, played a major role in exerting quality controls. Consequently, although there are academic boards analogous to university senates, faculty boards are less common. Indeed, although the polytechnics are much younger than universities, the role of the CNAA and their independent origins have allowed variety in their managerial structures.

Senates and academic boards

Notwithstanding the wide differences between university senates and PSHE academic boards, they have in common that they are the senior academic committees of their institutions; they usually have among their members all heads of academic departments and they are chaired by the institution's senior academic, namely, the Vice-Chancellor, Director or Principal. Their powers vary, but university senates are the supreme governing body in all academic matters. To maintain academic standards it is their job to stipulate academic policies and procedures. Senates are the final court of appeal on academic matters. Reflecting greater central control in polytechnics and colleges, academic boards are more likely to discuss academic policies than university senates.

The range of issues senates and academic boards may consider is enormous. The agenda may include discussion of recent government reports, reviews of fees, internal promotions, regulations for degrees and diplomas, consideration for honorary degrees, reports of examiners, staff development, the terms and conditions of academic appointments, regulations on student residence, standards for student admissions, the provision of journals in the library, laboratory safety, a programme of public lectures, the establishment of a science park or commercial company using academic consultants, reports from faculty boards, the Open Day and the provision of audio-visual aids, together with any number of matters that might not be regarded as academic at all, such as reports of the Building Committee, the Finance Committee and the problems of parking cars.

From this range of activities it will be clear that senates

and academic boards often have many sub-committees which predigest issues before submission to senate.

The inclusion of non-academic matters on the agendas of senates, and to a lesser extent of academic boards, reflects an important fact. During the period of expansion from 1964 to 1981 the power of academic staff steadily, but almost imperceptibly grew, while the influence of members of the community on university courts and councils waned. The numbers of junior lecturers on senates also grew and since 1968 there is usually some student representation. The period of stringency in the 1980s resulted in a swing back of power to Vice-Chancellors and university courts and was explicitly recommended by the Jarratt Committee of 1985 (see Chapter 3). When more draconian decisions were required, Vice-Chancellors took them and sought the support of their courts.

In one way the opposite could be said to have happened in the public sector (PSHE). PSHE institutions used to be dependent on local government finance and their governing bodies included many councillors. Since the Education Reform Act 1988 established the polytechnics as independent corporations and the academic control of the CNAA has been loosened, the power of academic boards in the public sector has been strengthened.

Another interpretation is to say that in both universities and in PSHE the central figure – the Vice-Chancellor, Director or Principal – has acquired more power. Yet both interpretations are illusory. It is the government that has taken more power.

How the money comes and goes

We have seen in Chapters 3 and 4 that universities and the public sector get their money in different ways. Universities get about one-third of their money in research contracts and the rest mostly from students' fees and the Universities Funding Council (UFC). The UFC gets it from the Department of Education and Science (DES).

Table 11.1   Income of Muncaster University

Recurrent income	£	%
	(in thousands)	
Exchequer grants (UFC)	21,000	42
Home full-time student fees	8,000	16
Overseas full-time student fees	2,000	4
Part-time course fees	300	0.6
Research, training and other support grants	150	0.3
Endowments, donations and subscriptions	550	1.1
Computer Board grants	350	0.7
Other general recurrent income	1,650	3.3
Total general recurrent income	34,000	68
Research grants and contracts	11,400	22.8
Income for other services rendered	2,600	5.2
Specific income	14,000	28
Total recurrent income	48,000	96
Non-recurrent Exchequer grants		
Equipment and furniture	1,680	3.3
Building works	140	0.3
Purchase of sites and properties	4	
Professional fees	36	0.1
Teaching hospitals	140	0.3
Total non-recurrent income	2,000	4
Total income	50,000	100

We saw that in the public sector institutions get their money from students' fees and the Polytechnics and Colleges Funding Council (PCFC). Polytechnics that have obtained corporate status do so under contractual relationships while others continue to receive grants until they attain that status. The PCFC gets its money from a central pool fed by contributions from local authorities. Public sector institutions get some money from research contracts, but not a lot, though the sum may be increasing.

Of course that is a simplified description and it gives no indication of how the money is spent or the size of the budgets.

To do this let us look at the income and expenditure accounts of an imaginary university, Muncaster. It is a little larger than average and has a medical school. I have obtained its accounts by assuming income and expenditure are each £50 million a year and that the proportions under each heading are roughly similar to those for all universities. I have then rounded the figures so that they can be digested more easily. Actually, owing to the severity of cuts in funding, most universities are eating into their reserves at present – their expenditure exceeds their income, but by the early 1990s they expect to be in balance.

Starting from the bottom of Table 11.1, you will see that about 4 per cent of its income is from one-off (non-recurrent) grants from the UFC for special equipment for research and buildings.

Table 11.2 Estimated annual cost per student of courses in 1990

	£
Mathematics and statistics	2,700
Business and administrative studies	2,800
Humanities (excluding archaeology)	2,800
Languages and related disciplines	2,900
Mass communication and documentation	2,900
Archaeology	3,100
Computer studies	3,100
Creative arts	3,300
Education	3,500
Architecture, building and planning	3,800
Subjects allied to medicine	4,000
Agriculture (excluding veterinary science)	4,200
Biological sciences	4,300
Physical sciences	4,600
Pre-clinical medicine	4,600
Engineering and technology	4,700
Pre-clinical dentistry	5,200
Veterinary science	8,100
Clinical medicine	8,500
Clinical dentistry	9,400

Table 11.3 **Expenditure of Muncaster University**

Recurrent expenditure	£ (in thousands)		%	
Academic departments				
Academic and related salaries	14,000		28	
Other salaries and wages	4,000		8	
Other expenditure	2,000		4	
Total general expenditure		20,000		40
Research grants and contracts	8,000		16	
Other services rendered	2,000		4	
Total specific expenditure		10,000		20
Total academic departments		30,000		60
Academic services				
Library	2,000		4	
Central university computer	1,000		2	
Other services	1,000		2	
Total academic services		4,000		8
Total general educational expenditure		1,000		2
Total administration and central services		2,500		5
Maintenance				
Rates	1,800		3.6	
Heat, light, power, water	1,400		2.8	
Repairs and maintenance	2,000		4	
Cleaning and custodial services	1,200		2.4	
Telephones	350		0.7	
Other	750		1.5	
Total maintenance and running of premises		7,500		15
Total staff and student facilities and amenities		1,000		2
Total pensions		500		1
Total capital expenditure from recurrent income		750		1.5
Other recurrent expenditure		500		1
Total recurrent expenditure		47,750		95.5
Non-recurrent expenditure				
Equipment	2,000		4	
Furniture	200		0.4	
Other	50		0.1	
		2,250		4.5
Total expenditure		50,000		100

At Muncaster, income for specific research contracts and services (28 per cent) is a little less than the average, but like all universities this proportion is steadily increasing and is expected to be 33 per cent or more in three to five years' time.

Turning to the general recurrent income, by far the largest sources are the UFC (£21 million), fees from full-time students normally resident in UK (£8 million), and fees from overseas students. Before 1990 when the government decided to raise students' fees from £607 to £1,600 and save Exchequer funds, these figures would have been £26 million and £3 million. From these figures you can work out that Muncaster has about 5,000 home-based students (£8 million divided by £1,600). It also has between 500 and 600 overseas students. These are students from outside the European Community who pay the full cost of their courses. Naturally the full cost of a course varies with the course. In Britain we are used to education on the cheap, or at least the true cost being hidden. Table 11.2 may help to set that right. Although parents may complain about what they have to pay to keep their son or daughter at university, in practice they get a pretty good bargain.

Turning now to expenditure shown in Table 11.3 it is possible to see straight away at the top that £18 million (£14m + £4m) is spent on salaries in the academic departments. These are recurrent salaries of permanent staff with annual increments. They amount to over half the general recurrent income (£34 million).

What else has to be paid out of that £34 million? The costs of the university library, the university computing centre, other central services such as audio-visual technicians and the language centre, the central administration of the university, examinations, extra-mural classes, the maintenance of buildings including porters and security staff – in fact everything except expenses for which there are specific funds such as research contracts and capital (non-recurrent) expenditure. In fact the £34 million is not enough.

The university would not break even if it were not for its specific income. That is its £14 million income from research contracts and other services. Its expenditure on these contracts and services is only £10 million. The other £4 million is spent on overheads. But the university would have to pay most of those overheads (maintenance, administration, academic services etc.) anyway. So without the research overheads the university would be in the red.

That, in a nutshell, is the pressure under which universities live. It needs spelling out because many people think that universities survive on grants from the government and do not have to live with market forces like the worlds of commerce and industry. They do.

It might be thought that the public sector does not live under this pressure because it does not pursue research to the same extent. That is not true. Research income has given the universities some financial flexibility. The public sector has always been less well off and it shows in the state of its buildings and in the class sizes and time pressures in which its staffs have to work.

The management of every industry is different from others in some respects arising from the nature of their business. Likewise the management of higher education has its own characteristics and problems.

Further reading

Geoffrey Lockwood and John Davies, *Universities: the management challenge* (Society for Research into Higher Education, 1985).

Chapter 12

WHAT ARE ACADEMICS REALLY LIKE?

Some misleading impressions

It is quite common for members of the general public to think that academics come from professional families, were sent to fee-paying schools, showed academic brilliance throughout their school days, going on to Oxbridge where they all distinguished themselves with first-class honours degrees, went straight from being a student to being a lecturer and have political views to the left of centre.

While there is an element of truth in some of these assertions, as a general picture it is wholly misleading. In one survey, about 60 per cent of university teachers had fathers whose occupation was classified as in social classes I and II, but the proportion in the public sector higher education (PSHE) might be lower. About a fifth of university teachers had been to a public school and that is more than for the population as a whole, but two-thirds came from grammar and direct grant schools (before the abolition of the 11-plus exam and the formation of comprehensive schools). The figures for polytechnic staff are not very different: around 15 per cent from public schools and 70 per cent from former grammar and direct grant schools.

More than 75 per cent of university lecturers have never studied at Oxbridge and the proportion in PSHE is over 90 per cent. Around 20 per cent in both universities and polytechnics have a London degree; while over half in the polytechnics and more than a quarter in universities went to one of the civic universities described in Chapter 4. Unfortunately, even in PSHE, the proportion of academic staff from the ex-CATS or with CNAA degrees is very small. The old pecking order still exists.

It is true that in the early 1960s just over half university staff had a first-class degree, but the figure fell to 37 per cent during the rapid expansion in the late 1960s and early 1970s.

In 1973 only 13 per cent of staff who taught on degree courses in polytechnics had a first, and another 33 per cent had an upper second-class degree. Over a third had a master's degree and more than a fifth, a doctorate. I don't know a more recent survey, but these proportions are almost certainly higher now. By any criterion the academic quality of polytechnics has continued to rise throughout their short history.

It should be remembered that at the time that most polytechnic teachers trained, there were no degrees awarded anywhere in many of the subjects they teach. Hence comparisons with universities in the last two paragraphs should be viewed with care. The experience and professionalism of polytechnic staff in the 1970s was shown by the fact that over two-thirds had professional qualifications and 82 per cent had degrees. Only 14 per cent had come 'straight from college'. Furthermore 25 per cent had qualifications in teaching compared with only 19 per cent in universities. The same was true of the ex-CATs at a comparable stage in their development. In the former colleges of education the proportion with both academic and professional qualifications has always been higher.

As far as political leanings are concerned, judging from a survey published at the time of the last election and another twenty years ago, it would seem that academic voting habits swing with those for the rest of the country. There may be a tendency to the left, but there is reason to think that there was a greater proportion voting for the centre parties than in the country as a whole.

The changing composition of British academe

The changing age distribution

We're getting older. Table 12.1 shows the distribution of university academic staff by age and rank in 1989. The age distribution reflects the years of expansion from 1964 to 1981. Either side of those dates relatively few staff were recruited. Typically members of academic staff are recruited in their late twenties or early thirties when they have had around ten years' experience of the world, yet still have a freshness of mind to do original research.

The bunching of staff in their forties also reflects stringent staffing policies since the cuts in 1981. Early retirement schemes were introduced for the over-fifties. Furthermore, since that date nearly 20 per cent of academic staff under the age of 30 leave in any given year while the corresponding figure before 1981 was only 1 per cent. The university lecturer scale is a long one with annual increments in salary for seventeen years. Consequently universities cannot afford to appoint young staff on permanent contracts and most of the best brains drain away after contracts of three to five years just when their potential is coming into flower and they have learnt enough to take further responsibilities.

The distribution also reflects patterns of promotion. Most lecturers must wait until their forties before they are promoted. Many don't get it even then and a good proportion in their fifties have taken advantage of early retirement schemes.

Table 12.1 Full-time non-clinical academic staff in British universities in 1989 analysed by age group and rank

Age	Professors		Readers and senior lecturers		Lecturers		Others		Total	
	No.	%	No.	%	No.	%	No.	%	No.	%
Under 25	–	–	–	–	94	48	101	52	195	1
25–29	1	0	2	0	1,079	86	170	14	1,252	5
30–34	10	0	42	2	2,305	95	81	3	2,438	9
35–39	132	3	489	13	3,161	83	34	1	3,816	14
40–44	446	8	1,435	26	3,610	65	26	0	5,517	20
45–49	742	13	1,966	35	2,823	51	20	0	5,551	20
50–54	861	19	1,840	41	1,775	40	8	0	4,484	16
55–59	665	27	979	39	834	34	4	0	2,482	9
over 59	585	39	473	32	436	29	5	0	1,499	5
Totals	3,442	13	7,226	26	16,117	59	449	2	27,234	100

Percentages are rounded to the nearest whole number.
Source: Universities Statistical Record.

There is an extra grade of lecturer in the polytechnics and the scales are shorter. They have lecturers, senior lecturers and principal lecturers. An increasing number of polytechnics award the titles Reader and Professor to members of staff distinguished in research. The yardstick is comparability with the universities.

There is a similar age bunching in the public sector (PSHE) but it is less acute and the reasons are slightly different. The period of expansion was greatest a little later (in the early 1970s when the polytechnics were first established), but on the whole polytechnic staff have had a little longer in other jobs before taking up teaching. So the same age group was trawled for staff. The cutback in local authority spending in the 1980s meant that PSHE had to implement similar staffing policies.

These policies have resulted in a widening generation gap between the students of today and their teachers. Parents should not assume that staff–student relationships are the same as they were in their day.

The changing sources of finance

There's less government money now. Thirty-five per cent of university academic staff are not wholly financed by their university. They are financed by industry or by research grants. Ten years earlier the figure was 19 per cent. In fact in the ten years before 1989 the number of full-time staff not wholly university financed more than doubled (114 per cent) while the number of full-time staff wholly financed by the universities fell by 7 per cent. The proportion of PSHE staff primarily engaged in independently funded research is much smaller. Consequently PSHE has been much more dependent on government finance, either at a local or national level.

How many part-timers are there?

They are too few, and of the wrong kind. The number of part-time teaching and research staff has never been great (4 per cent) and it has recently begun to fall. But in the years after the 1981 cuts it rose significantly (by 88 per cent). The rise may herald a greater dependence on part-time staff which might also lead to a different style of relationships between students and their teachers. Much of the increase consisted of staff who retired early and then continued to do some part-time work to plug the gaps they left behind. What higher education needs is more part-time staff who work elsewhere and who use that experience creatively to cross-fertilise perspectives and generate new lines of thought.

The poor but improving balance of female staff

There are too few women in education and certainly too few in senior positions. Table 12.2 shows the proportion of women employed as academics. It shows that the percentage at all levels is well below the proportion of women in the population as a whole and is below the proportion of undergraduates. From student to professor men appear to be relatively favoured. However the scene is changing. Since 1978 the proportion of women appointed has increased at all levels and whether or not the posts have been wholly university financed. Indeed, so far as university-financed staff are concerned, since 1978 at every level there has been a reduction in the number of men and an increase in the number of women.

Table 12.2 The percentage, in 1989, of full-time academic staff in universities (Great Britain) who were women

	University financed	Not wholly university financed	Total
Professors	3	6	3
Readers/SL	7	17	8
Lecturers	17	27	21
Others	51	40	41
Total (1989)	13	30	19
Total (1978)	10	22	12

Percentages are rounded to the nearest whole number.
Source: Universities Statistical Record.

In the public sector of higher education (PSHE) the distribution of the sexes is dominated by the disciplines. Thus former colleges of education have large numbers of female staff, while engineering departments have few. Overall the balance of the sexes is little different in PSHE from in the universities.

Understanding how academics think

They think in different ways. But what ways? Academic staff think of themselves as physicists, engineers, historians, biologists, geographers, chemists and so on. They do not, in their work, primarily think of themselves as members of their university, college or polytechnic. In everyday life it is loyalty to their group that is required, not loyalty to their wider institution. Where the subject group is large, their self-image becomes even more specific. They see themselves as physical or human geographers and organic or inorganic chemists. In a really large department they may split further so that among physical geographers, climatologists only have passing contact with geomorphologists.

The reason often given is that academics researching in a given field need to discuss their work with others who understand it. That may be true to a point, but in most institutions there could usefully be more cross-departmental interaction on intellectual issues than there is. The crucial factor is one about human beings: they cannot run more than six or seven close working relationships in any one environment and most people manage fewer than that. The same is true in factories or anywhere else.

Because group influence is so strong, academics working together develop certain common ways of thinking. For example, the marks of two examiners from the same department will correlate more highly than two in the same discipline from different institutions. They make the same kinds of judgements because they tend to think along the same lines. They ask themselves the same kind of questions and tend to use the same kinds of explanation. They have to, or they wouldn't understand each other.

But in reality lots of things can be explained in many different ways. A given question is capable of different kinds of answer, all of which are correct in their own terms. So in selecting one kind of explanation academics neglect others.

If I give a lot of examples you will see that each discipline uses several types of explanation. The study of literature includes understanding the author's intention, the function of language, the development of a plot, the morals and values involved, grammatical rules and an overall experience of a work. Biology is also concerned with function and development (of organisms, not novels, poems or plays). It also considers the spatial arrangement of anatomical structures, cause and effect, and the mathematical laws of inheritance. But morals, intentions and experience are seen as being too subjective for science. Physics, too, is strong on cause and effect, spatial structures and mathematical rules. Philosophers use logical (not just mathematical) rules and their experience. Economists explain the cost of goods as a function of supply and demand. They use mathematical rules to do it. Sociologists also talk about the functions of marriage. Psychologists explain behaviour in terms of intentions (motivation), child development, experience, biological functions, the structure of the brain and so on. This list could be lengthened.

The point is that there are certain types of explanation that are used across many disciplines. They explain in terms of: spatial structure, development over time, rules or laws, cause and effect, functional relationships, intentions (purposes), values (including moral values), and personal experience. These overlap.

Any academic uses several types of explanation while having preferences (which may be unconscious). Academics in the same small group will explain things in the same way. Few disciplines use all types of explanation, and most will reject some types as inappropriate. Disciplines can make sudden big advances by looking at new kinds of explanation (e.g. the study of human intentions to explain geographical facts) or by rejecting old ones (e.g. spiritual revelation and astrology).

This is a very brief account of the ways different academics think. As it requires the reader to look down, godlike, upon the thought patterns of some of the nation's best intellects, he or she may find that it requires rereading and a lot of thought.

It can also be used by parents to appreciate their children's intellectual development at college. When students go to college they are trained to understand things in some ways more than in others. In short they get particular perspectives on life. The perspectives may be different from those of their parents. Higher education for one member of a family is an opportunity for all to widen their horizons. Unfortunately in practice, different perspectives often lead to interpersonal barriers, rather than opening new vistas.

What makes a good academic?

It all depends how, and what, you evaluate. Academics undertake research, teaching and management. Some do more of one than another, but in universities the overall ratios are supposed to be around 40:40:20. One survey found that university lecturers worked an average of 50.5 hours per week, with senior lecturers working 2 hours, and professors 4 hours, more. This implies a little over 20 hours each on teaching and research. Another report suggested 42 hours per week with rather less spent on research than teaching, and 35 hours a week by staff in polytechnics, with an average of only 3 hours on research. In the Central Institutions of Scotland 35 hours a week on matters to do with teaching is a notional norm (this includes time for marking, preparation and so on). Research time has to be additional. However the quantity of time spent does not necessarily indicate the quality of the work done.

There is a common belief that the quality of an academic's research can be judged, but the quality of teaching cannot. Promotion criteria, particularly in universities, are heavily weighted towards research in consequence. This is a mistake. Teaching can be evaluated, but neither is easy. There are no adequate measurements. All one can do is to gather evidence that gives an indication of quality (indicators). No one indicator is sufficient for either.

How are researchers assessed?

Mostly by their publications. The quality of research is judged by fellow academics, journal editors and publishers' advisers before it is published; and it is then reviewed, criticised or cited afterwards. It is assumed that these judges use criteria appropriate to the subject, such as whether the findings will stand the test of time, whether the methods are original and could be replicated, whether interpretations of the facts are reasonable, whether it will stimulate new work and so on. So the amount published and, more rarely, the number of citations have been used as indicators of the quality of an academic's research.

Such data are available, but they have their limitations. If promotion were dependent on the number of articles published, academics might be tempted to publish many short superficial articles in less reputable journals. Promotion decisions often involve comparing lecturers in different departments, but cross-discipline comparisons can be very misleading. Journal space varies with the subject. So do conventions of co-authorship. If a chemistry PhD student publishes his work it is common practice for the supervisor to attach his name as co-author. In arts subjects that would be very unusual. Furthermore, a reasonable publication rate will vary with the nature of the work. A scholarly article in philosophy or literature may take years to work out and write; while an article reporting some experimental research could take only two or three months from conception to completion. ('Scholarship' involves the reinterpretation of information already known; while 'research' involves a procedure to discover new information.)

Citation data are necessarily delayed. Authors of highly original work may not be quoted very much because it is difficult to understand or because it is not in the mainstream of current work. Again, there are subject differences. Citation is used more in the humanities than in the physical sciences partly because the latter are more quantitative, less dependent on context for their interpretation and less controversial.

One way over these difficulties when judging who is a good academic, is to consult others in the same field. This is known as 'peer review'. Peers, it is said, will be able to make a subjective judgement on the quality of research and scholarship published taking all the variables into account. The big question with peer review is to decide who the peers should be. If only a few are consulted their influence, not to say their prejudices, would be very influential. Peers in other institutions are often rivals for funding. The unfair influence of individuals can be offset by consulting a large number of peers, but that is expensive and time-consuming.

More recently measures based on the amount of research

funding obtained have been used; but this, too, is not a very fair indicator of who is doing a good job. Funding is subject to the whims of fashion and current policies of grant-awarding bodies. Research topics, even within the same subject, vary greatly in expense. The Research Councils (which sponsor research) could be influenced by an inner circle of researchers each scratching each other's back. There have been frequent complaints that, owing to government pressure, those engaged in fundamental research have been penalised compared with those whose research is more applied.

How can the quality of teaching be judged?

By using many indicators. Most promotion committees use too few. Universities don't evaluate teaching enough; but a variety of indicators have long been used in public sector higher education (PSHE) by Her Majesty's Inspectors and, at the time of course validation and review, by the Council for National Academic Awards.

Indicators can be classified under four groups of questions: 'What are the consequences of the teaching?', 'What opinions are there about it?', 'How can the teacher's techniques be described?' and 'What resources are used?'

The consequences include the quality of students' work in assignments, presentations and examinations, and their attendance at classes. It is possible to observe how students develop on a course or to compare their development with those on other courses either at the time or some time later.

Opinions may be sought from students, the teacher's colleagues, staff development officers, inspectors and the teacher himself by the use of questionnaires or interviews. Each of these groups obtained their opinions in different ways. There are other indicators of opinions, for example the number of students who choose to take a teacher's optional course or who withdraw from it. Some form of opinion collection is by far the most common technique. The observations on which the opinions are based and the techniques of collecting them vary a great deal (e.g. the design of questionnaires or how far interviews are structured). A very great deal of research has been done on students' opinions of teaching. There is no doubt that people are very consistent in the opinions they hold, but it remains doubtful how far they are valid when compared with more objective observations.

Techniques to describe what a teacher does are always selective. They include observing the teaching, or video-recording it for later analysis, analysing critical incidents in the classroom, conducting case studies, keeping diaries, looking at the teacher's records and an analysis of the teacher's workload.

An inventory of the resources used by a teacher cannot, on its own, be used to judge the quality of teaching; but it can help to build up a picture. Copies of reading lists, instructions for student assignments, handouts, and a record of visual aids and other equipment used in teaching can all give an indication of a teacher's style.

The first serious attempts to find ways to evaluate teaching were concerned with the individual teacher, his or her improvement and promotion. They assumed that the quality of teaching is reflected in the amount students learn and the behaviour of the teacher. Psychologists study learning and behaviour. Accordingly the methods of psychologists are prominent in those I have just described.

Judging the quality of departments

More recently the funding councils have been asking the question 'Which departments are most worth funding?' So attention has also turned to the evaluation of departments, and their value has been seen more in terms of money and economic benefits, rather than in human terms. As a result the methods of economists are more prominent. From the point of view of economists there are two forms of production by academic departments: research findings and qualified labour.

To judge the quality of a department's research, prominence has been given to the number of its research students, its research income, its five best publications, its reputation among others in the same field and the products of research such as patents and industrial applications. In fact university funding has recently been adjusted so that departments seen as above average in terms of research have earned 10 per cent more cash than their number of students would justify; and those judged below average have earned 10 per cent less.

To judge the quality of a department's teaching consideration has been given to the value added to the worth of a student. For example a department producing students with good degree results either at a low cost per student or when the entry qualifications of students were low, might be said to be giving good value for money. The popularity of a department among student applicants, the proportion who drop out during the course and the number who get jobs on completion have all been suggested as indicators of teaching quality by economists; but it takes little thought to realise that a whole range of social factors might better explain such data. The use of student and peer review has also been suggested, but to think that people in one institution will judge their teachers, not only on the same criteria, but with the same degree of strictness or leniency as those in another, is facile. There has been no adjustment of university finance on the basis of the quality of teaching.

None the less the Funding Councils are probably right to try to use a variety of criteria, since no single criterion could be satisfactory. They are looking for quantitative criteria to justify the amount of money they give, but in the end there is a truism they cannot escape: the qualities of teaching and research are qualitative, not quantitative.

The growth of formal staff appraisal

Contrary to common opinion, academics are constantly being judged. What is more, those judgements have always been a powerful influence on their behaviour and promotion. Reputation, not money, is what motivates academics. They also value freedom in the way they work. However, appraisal has not always been regular and systematic. Partly in response to financial threats from the government, much more systematic appraisal has been introduced into most institutions of higher education in the late 1980s.

These systems of appraisal usually involve an annual review meeting for each individual with his or her immediate superior. Typically they will set targets for the coming year and review how far the previous year's targets have been achieved. What is discussed is usually confidential, but to a point, an academic's targets have to be known by his immediate colleagues, and in many institutions it is accepted that the superior may use a record of the appraisal process when reporting to the Promotions Committee.

Staff development in higher education

There is no point in evaluating academic staff and their departments if, having done so, there is no back-up service for improvements. University teaching in particular has been criticised for centuries, but until recently, in contrast to school teachers, no training has been given.

Arguably there has been some staff development in research. Departmental research seminars, conferences, the refereeing of research proposals by grant-awarding bodies, and reading critical reviews of research are all activities where the highest standards are constantly being reasserted, often at a remarkable degree of detail.

How staff development activities have grown

The government first expressed its concern about university teaching methods in the Hale Report of 1964. Students, too, repeatedly argued for the training of university teachers and in 1966, the first unit of its kind, the University Teaching Methods Research Unit, was established in London. It ran short courses, particularly for new academic staff; and by the early 1970s appointments for staff development were made at several universities, including Exeter, Salford, Aston, Bradford, Nottingham and Birmingham. There was also vigorous activity at Surrey and Loughborough. The Nuffield Foundation funded a unit to publicise innovations in higher education. In 1973 the Committee of Vice-Chancellors appointed a Co-ordinating Officer for the Training of University Teachers, but they withdrew funding in 1979. Indeed, hardly any of these initiatives survived the 1980s. Why?

There was considerable resistance to staff development activities in the universities. The reason was not only that the need for staff development seemed to imply that senior staff had not been doing their job satisfactorily for many years, but that teaching essentially involves developing personal relationships. That is a very sensitive area in which to develop self-awareness in the presence of one's colleagues, particularly for people who have hardly ever experienced serious failure. The privacy of the classroom had preserved teaching as a private matter. Senior staff feared exposure, but could not say so in case they seemed to be trying to hide a weakness.

Staff development was better accepted in the polytechnics. Many had appointed staff development officers, usually by some other name. The staff had a different attitude. This was partly because they had to justify the quality of their courses to the CNAA and partly because they had a heritage with closer links to industries where formalised staff training is normal. (It is not a coincidence that five of the nine universities mentioned in the paragraph before last, were ex-CATs having the same heritage as the polytechnics.) The Standing Conference for Educational Development Services in Polytechnics (SCEDSIP) was established and now (renamed SCED) includes staff developers from all sections of higher education.

In spite of resistance in universities, it was during the 1970s that the methods of staff development which are now commonplace, were being explored and refined. Four broad strategies evolved.

Development by making staff better informed

The first strategy is to do research into higher education and to disseminate information through the in-house publications or by whatever means is available. This is an academically respectable path. It includes using research methods to evaluate an individual's teaching confidentially at his or her request. Research takes time. A lone staff developer cannot serve many staff by this strategy, and information alone is slow to change attitudes. But in the long run this strategy is an essential component for staff development.

Staff development through conventional short courses

The second strategy is to run formal courses of a fairly conventional type with talks on specific topics, such as 'student assessment', given by 'experts', followed by discussion. Such courses are open to all and serve large numbers if they care to come. The most common topics are small group teaching, lecturing, computer-based learning, personal tutoring, helping students to learn, assessment of students, research supervision and evaluating teaching.

Unfortunately, with even quite small numbers, both the talks and the discussion tend to cover only general issues and rarely get to the heart of each individual's personal needs, unless a participant has the courage to raise them. Furthermore, merely talking about problems does not necessarily result in action though arguably it is a necessary first step.

Developing attitudes and inter-personal awareness in support groups

A totally different style is analogous to co-counselling. The staff developer works initially with a small group of friendly colleagues developing close and trusted relationships. A supportive group provides members with confidence to express their concerns about teaching and in which to develop the self-awareness of inter-personal skills that is so important in teaching. Gradually the network of friendships widens and support in the institution grows. This approach, like the first one, is slow to bear fruit. It requires considerable inter-personal skill.

Training in skills

A fourth approach is to see teaching as a whole lot of skills, from how to explain a concept to how to arrange the furniture for a discussion. Advocates of this approach developed workshop techniques in which participants practised various skills, were given feedback on their performance and then tried to perform them better. Video-recordings are a natural aid; and it is a short step from using the cameras in special workshop sessions, to taking them into the lecture theatre for thorough analysis afterwards, either privately, with the help of the staff developer, or in the presence of some of the students as well. Obviously this approach requires teachers to be able to face themselves, but once they have done so, their appreciation of the method is strong. To assist with particular skills the method is quick; but not all aspects of teaching can easily be analysed in terms of specifiable skills.

What is the future of higher education?

I can only speculate, but change looks certain.

Its purposes

I think change will more and more be driven by finance unless governments can take a wider view of what is important. As a result 'instruction in occupational skills' and financial objectives will increasingly suffocate less tangible aims. Values to do with people's feelings, thoughts, learning and social relations (the other purposes covered in Chapter 2) will not be squeezed out entirely, because they are the foundations of occupational skills. But they are foundations for the rest of life too, not just our working lives.

Finance

It seems clear that institutions both sides of the binary line will depend much more on contract funding. Many more staff will be on short-term contracts. There is even a danger that institutions may wish to keep their research findings secret in order to exploit them commercially, rather than publish them for all to use freely. A pecking order between institutions will replace elite groups.

Who will have access to higher education?

Short courses for mature students, particularly employees, rather than full-time non-stop courses for 18-year-olds are likely to grow in importance. Industry will want academic credit for their employees who take courses and for those who don't need to. So credit accumulation schemes, modular courses, credit transfer and academic awards for learning from professional experience will be developed.

Learning methods and course design

This means that academe will need to market itself and tailor-make what it provides for the specific needs of its customers. Course design will become a process of negotiation. Paradoxically the burden of this process, the time it will take, will force academics to adapt and package together material prepared, tried and tested by others. Institutions will buy modular teaching material from each other. Individuals and departments will not only have reputations for their research, but for their teaching materials also. This could lead to a new kind of 'publish or perish'. The Open University has a head-start here.

Research

The involvement of industry in teaching and the growth of project work in schools will create new opportunities for research-based teaching at undergraduate level, but academics may be slow to see its possibilities. Increasing dependence upon industry will mean that more research is applied, using well-established techniques, and less will be fundamental using innovatory methods.

Staff development

Contract employment will broaden staff development services. I expect committee skills, marketing and entrepreneurial skills, skills in staff appraisal, helping overseas students and course design will receive more attention in the 1990s. That does not mean that staff development work will not continue to concentrate on teaching. The quality of teaching will grow in importance and the certification of teachers will be introduced. In 1989 the Committee of Vice-Chancellors and Principals once again established a central Staff Development and Training Unit and it could have an important role to play.

Conclusion

Higher education has many strands. At any time some are in tension and some are in harmony. That makes its organisation adaptable and its work creative. Understanding higher education requires seeing how all the strands interplay.

Further Reading

A. H. Halsey and Martin Trow, *The British Academics* (Faber and Faber, 1971).

INDEX